D0950529

A Concise History of the Hawaiian Islands

A
Concise History
of the
Hawaiian Islands

Dr. Phil Barnes

Dedication

This book is dedicated to the residents of Hawai'i's of all races who are working together to expand the spirit of aloha into the dawn of the new millenium.

Front Cover:
Kapa background is from a classic 19ᵗʰ Century kapa.

Paintings: *Voyage of Tradition* and *The Village of Ka'anapali*
© by Edwin Kayton / www.kayton-art.com

President Barack Obama photo courtesy of the White House
www.whitehouse.gov

Volcano photo *Rift Zone*
© by G. Brad Lewis / www.volcanoman.com

Back Cover:
View of Karakakooa Bay in Owyhee, Where Captn. Cook was Killed
from "Banke's New System of Geography,
published by Royal Authority"

Mahalo to Edwin Kayton and Brad Lewis for their generous permission to feature their stunning work on the front cover.

ISBN 978-0-912180-70-0

Published in Hawai'i by the Petroglyph Press, Ltd.
160 Kamehameha Avenue - Hilo, Hawai'i 96720
Phone (808) 935-6006 - Fax (808) 935-1553
PetroglyphPress@hawaiiantel.net
www.PetroglyphPress.com

First Edition 1999 ~ Eleven Printings
Second Edition 2009 ~ Two Printings
Third Edition - March 2013

Preface

My goal in writing this book was to create a short book that travelers to Hawai'i can read in a few hours. One's travels become more meaningful when viewed within the context of a historical framework. Many archaeological remains of pre-historic times can still be observed on all of the Hawaiian islands. Rich collections of early artifacts are not only found in museums but hotel lobbies. The Hawaiian Renaissance is much more than a marketing strategy for attracting visitors. Real change is in the air in the Hawaiian islands. This should be viewed as an exciting expansion of the aloha spirit rather than a threat to the status quo. May your appreciation of the cultural and environmental kaleidoscope of these beautiful islands be expanded by spending a bit of time in digesting this book. I have included a suggested reading materials list should you wish to expand your knowledge base.

On the 10th anniversary of the first printing of *A Concise History of the Hawaiian Islands,* in 2009 the book was updated as a second edition. New material and images have been added in several chapters as well as a new chapter to bring the book into the 21st century. The third edition includes additional minor revisions and additions. These are exciting times in Hawai'i and I strive to bring you up to date on the most recent happenings in our islands.

I would like to thank my wife, Diane, for her support. I would also like to thank my daughter, Dr. Brooke Barnes, for extensive editorial assistance. Bob Voris and Dr. Beth Hartley are also thanked for their reviews of early drafts. David and Christine Reed at Petroglyph Press have provided invaluable assistance in all of the updates and new material that are included in the second and third editions. Thanks to Bobby Camara for assistance in fact checking and historical accuracy. Most of all I would like to thank the Hawaiian people for their perseverance against exceptional odds to keep the feeling of aloha alive in these islands that I love.

Phil Barnes

Contents

Prologue

The Hawaiian Archipelago is one of the most remote groups of islands on the face of the planet. The Islands are over 2,400 miles from the closest continental land mass. This relative isolation has resulted in unique life forms and also accounts for the fact that the islands were one of the last spots on the globe to be populated.

The islands are all volcanic in origin with the youngest islands being on the southeast region of the chain. The islands are located on the Pacific plate. The plate moves slowly to the northwest. There is a hot spot that is stationary in the middle of the Pacific Ocean. This hot spot is actually a large vent where molten material flows to the surface. New islands are created in the southeast as the older islands slowly drift to the northwest. The island of Hawai'i, the newest island, is presently located over this hot spot. It emerged above the ocean surface less than one million years ago. It is the only Hawaiian island that still has active volcanoes. A new island, Lō'ihi, is forming to the southeast of the Island of Hawai'i. It is still 3,000 feet underwater and will not break the surface for thousands of years.

Volcanic activity is still much in evidence on the island of Hawai'i. Of the five volcanoes that formed this island two, Kīlauea and Mauna Loa, are still active. Mauna Loa last erupted in 1984. The east rift zone of Kīlauea has been erupting almost continuously since 1983. Over 200 homes in this region as well as countless historical and ecologically unique areas have been covered over by these flows. Check with the staff at Hawai'i Volcanoes National Park or at their website *www.nps.gov/havo* for current eruption information.

Erosion and island sinking are constant forces at work here, as well as elsewhere on the planet. The oldest islands in the Hawaiian Archipelago, such as French Frigate Shoals, are little more than coral heads a few feet above water at high tide. The sea and other elements have been reducing their size since the moment their volcanoes became dormant. The northwest Hawaiian islands are uninhabited and are currently a refuge for nesting sea birds, sea turtles, and Hawaiian monk seals. Designated Papahānaumokuākea Marine National Monument, they are under the jurisdiction of the U.S. Fish and Wildlife Service and all access other than scientific research is severely limited. At the other end of the chain are the mountains Mauna Kea and Mauna Loa on the island of Hawai'i which rise almost 14,000 feet above sea level, with peaks often covered in snow. Erosive factors and sinking have not had time to make dramatic inroads in this young island. Dramatic illustrations of this erosive principal are the Na Pali coast on Kaua'i and the north shore of Moloka'i, which contains the highest sea cliffs on earth. These sea cliffs or pali were created when massive chunks of the islands slid into the ocean during major earthquakes.

Hawaiian
Islands

There are eight major islands among the thousands of islands that compose the Hawaiian Archipelago . These are in order from east to west: Hawai'i, Maui, Kaho'olawe, Lāna'i, Moloka'i, O'ahu, Kaua'i, and Ni'ihau. These islands are all inhabited except for Kaho'olawe which was used by the U.S. Navy for years as a bombing range. It has been returned to the Hawaiian people and is being restored to its natural state. The size and elevation of these islands vary greatly. The island of Hawai'i is so large that all the other islands can fit into its boundary with lots of room to spare.

Since the islands are so isolated, life forms were slow to develop and have evolved into a unique biota. All life forms arrived on the islands by means of one of the three W's. Wave action carried many life forms, particularly flowering plants, to the islands. Anyone who has seen a coconut sprouting on the shore can appreciate this form of plant dispersal. Wings are the second means of introduction. Obviously birds arrived in the region, both the pelagic sea birds who travel the earth's oceans and land based birds who made it to the islands in powerful storm winds. Birds deposited many seeds in their feces as well as bringing insects and other life forms that were lodged in their feathers. Wind is the third natural pathway for the introduction of new species, particularly the high altitude jet stream that carries a heavy load of spores and other microscopic life forms.

Obviously these methods of dispersal would severely limit the gene pool in Hawai'i. With relatively few representatives from any given species and few total species, life forms evolved from a limited base to fill the many diverse ecological niches in the islands. Single species evolved into a great number of different but related species. The Hawaiian Honey Creeper, a family of small birds, is a good example of this phenomenon. More than 40 separate species evolved from a single colonizer. Almost all of the species found on the islands when the first inhabitants arrived were endemic, found only in Hawai'i. The introduction rate of new species has increased dramatically since that time.

An unusual characteristic of the endemic fauna of Hawai'i is that only two mammals were found on the islands before the first Polynesians arrived. These were the monk seal and a species of bat. This created an ecosystem with a distinct lack of predators, one of the reasons that introduced species have had such a devastating effect on the native species of plants and animals. A good example of this is the introduction of the mongoose in 1883. The goal was to find a predator to keep the rat population in check. As it turns out rats are nocturnal and mongooses are diurnal so they seldom come in contact. To make matters worse, mongooses eat even more of the native bird eggs than the rats they were brought in to control. Since that time the state has created an elaborate system to prevent the introduction of further new species.

There were also no native species of reptiles and amphibians. Except for the earthworm-size blind snake, there are still no snakes in the wild on the islands. This situation is presently being tested by the brown tree snakes from Guam. This poisonous snake has a propensity to stow away on airplanes flying into Hawai'i. Efforts are being made to try to keep this new intruder from gaining a foothold in Hawai'i.

Chapter 1
First Settlement

Before looking at the arrival of the first humans in Hawai'i, an examination of the voyaging traditions of the Polynesians is in order. Although there is still a scholarly debate on the origins and migration of the Polynesian peoples, the dominant theory is that they migrated from Asia to the Southeast Asian Peninsula and then continued across the sea into Indonesia. From there they followed an easterly route across Melanesia and Micronesia to the vicinity of Fiji. From this juncture one strand headed south to New Zealand. Another headed north, through the Society Islands, to the Marquesas and then on to Hawai'i. This should not be interpreted as a mass migration. It was more a series of fairly short voyages over perhaps a thousand years. As with the history of all groups before the advent of writing, it is possible to establish a chronological sequence from the oral histories, but exact dates can not be given. As a side note, Polynesia is described as the region included in a triangle with the western corner being New Zealand, the eastern corner Easter Island, and the northern point Hawai'i.

What drove these nomads of the seas? How and why did they shove off into uncharted oceans? The easy answer is that, like all peoples of the hunter-gatherer tradition, they were constantly searching for food, but it is not this simple. They had a history of agriculture and food harvesting technologies that allowed them to harvest the surplus of food that is essential for a people to create the rich civilization that characterizes this region. It is undoubtedly true that, even with this abundance of food, an area would eventually no longer be able to support the expanding population and a group would be formed to head out to sea in search of new lands. Tribal conflict could also be resolved by the less powerful group going their own way rather than engaging in warfare.

These expeditions were well planned so that the group would have all of the necessities that they required when they

Pua'a ~ Hawaiian Pig

reached their new home. They would carry livestock in the form of chickens, dogs, and pigs. Plants such as bananas, taro, ti, coconut, sweet potatoes and breadfruit were taken to cultivate for future harvest. Medicinal plants would ensure necessary remedies for healing rituals. Food for the voyagers and their animals would be required as well as water both for themselves and to water their plants. Basic tools, cordage, gourds, and other supplies would need to be included.

Perhaps more important than the physical materials that were taken would be the makeup of the crew itself. There were commonly from 20 to 40 people on each vessel. Often three or four canoes would travel together. This would provide an added element of safety at sea as well as a larger group of colonists to form their society on the new island when they landed. There would need to be a cross section of males and females as well as members of diverse families to avoid the problems associated with inbreeding. Individuals would also need to possess the skills to establish their new habitation, as well as those skills needed to pilot a craft in unknown waters for an extended voyage. And not all voyagers successfully completed their journey. No one knows how many of these pioneers perished at sea before being able to make a landfall.

Their methods of navigating have been resurrected by Polynesians who wish to keep the voyaging traditions alive. This navigation was a combination of celestial observations such as marker stars at night and cloud formations during the day, as well as evaluating flotsam (objects floating in the water), bird and fish species that were sighted, current flow, etc.

As the number of floating objects increased and they sighted birds with limited flight range they would know that they were getting closer to land days before an actual sighting would be made. This was a complex system that involved no instruments and, since writing was not present, had to be learned by rote memory.

The voyaging vessels themselves could take several different forms. They consisted of hulls that were created by large hollowing out logs. These dugouts were then decked with shaped wood pieces made of woods indigenous to the island. The hollowed out area could then be used to store supplies in a dry environment. This hull would either be joined to a

Voyaging Canoe

similar hull to create a catamaran or have an outrigger attached to construct a stable and seaworthy craft. A platform was attached to the two hulls which created a living area for the voyagers. A small hut or shed roof was added for protection from the elements.

Vessels would be propelled by sails and maneuvered by steering paddles. These craft had the advantage of drawing far less water than the larger European sailing ships. It was thus much easier to navigate the dangerous coral shoals. The canoes could be paddled directly onto the beach rather than mooring a quarter mile out to sea. This allowed them to escape the destructive force of the not uncommon tropical storms.

It is commonly speculated that the first Polynesians to reach Hawai'i came from the Marquesas Islands in what is now French Polynesia. These islands are some of the most inhospitable in all of the South Pacific. The main islands are ringed by sea cliffs and divided by valleys that are so deep that the bottom receives little direct sunlight. Thus access to both the bounty of the ocean and arable land for farming was extremely limited. All in all, it is not hard to imagine why a group would want to strike out for a more accommodating environment. The Marquesas are over 1,000 miles from Hawai'i. That would make this one of the longest voyages over open ocean in all of Polynesia.

Wherever their origin, the first landfall is thought to have been on the southern coast of the island of Hawai'i. Again, there is a debate as to the time of this arrival. While some estimates have put this landing as early as 100 A.D, recent scholarship and new analytical methods have called into question some of the earlier dates and estimates of 1000-1200 A.D. are commonly accepted. If the voyagers were running low on supplies when they reached Hawai'i, the next group of islands to the north is the Aleutian Chain of Alaska. Mauna Loa may have been erupting at the time. At a height of 13,600 feet this beacon could be observed far out to sea, particularly at night. Even if the volcano was not erupting the great mass of the island's mountains creates its own weather system with clouds stacking up high into the sky. This would be a sign that the skillful navigators would not be likely to miss if they were even within 100 miles of the island.

Once a landfall was made they would quickly have gone to work to recreate the agricultural and domestic attributes of their homeland. They would of course be mindful of specific differences in their new surroundings and would modify their practices to adapt to the new environmental conditions. These original settlers perhaps had the islands to themselves for several centuries. During this time period they occupied all of the major islands in the Hawaiian chain. It is thought that around the year 1275 A.D. a large contingent arrived from the islands of Tahiti. These new arrivals were physically larger and quickly established their dominance over the original inhabitants. In a relatively short period of time a new hierarchy was created, with the Tahitians bringing a new chiefly and priestly class and the former occupants reduced to the role of commoners.

Since little is known of these smaller original inhabitants some say they are the basis of the Menehune mythology. These are the "little people" that come out only at night and are known for their engineering prowess. Many rock walls and other structures in the islands are attributed to their labor.

It is speculated that in the early years following the arrival of the Tahitians there was voyaging between Hawai'i and Tahiti with a wholesale migration of large numbers of Tahitians and trade between the two regions. For unknown reasons all contact with the rest of Polynesia suddenly ceased and the Hawaiian Islands remained isolated until the arrival of the Europeans almost 800 years later. It was during this time period that the rich culture of Hawai'i developed in a manner that allowed hundreds of thousands of inhabitants to exist in the islands with all of their physical needs being met with a minimum of difficulty. Their remaining free time could be devoted to all of those aspects of music, dance, and the arts that make Hawai'i such a compelling destination today.

Male Hula Dancers with Tattoo

14

Chapter 2
Pre-European Hawai'i

A complex system of government evolved in Hawai'i. Members of the ruling class were called ali'i. There was a broad variety of rank within the ali'i. High chiefs possessed absolute power, comparable to kings in other cultures. Kamehameha, in the early 1800's, was the first chief to unite the entire island

Warrior in a gourd helmet by John Webber

chain under one rule. Until that time there could be several ruling chiefs on the same island. This created a system of almost constant warfare, both between islands and within the larger islands. One of the first criteria for attaining status as an

15

ali'i, besides heritage, was being a powerful warrior. It should be noted that the ali'i actually led their troops into battle in a literal fashion. In some battles the whole fight would be between the ranking ali'i on the two sides. When not involved in an actual conflict the men would be practicing military skills and waging mock battles. One of the most admired attributes of a warrior was the ability to catch a spear that was hurled at him in mid-air. Kamehameha I was supposedly unsurpassed at this art.

One would think that all of this warfare would severely reduce the male population of the islands, but that was not the case. Most fighting was actually hand to hand combat carried on by a warrior class. A battle could go on for days with few casualties. Although many warriors were killed, the casualties could have been much higher, and were once Western weapons and techniques arrived on the scene.

As well as prowess in battle, ancestral rank was a critical factor in establishing status as an ali'i. This is why genealogy was extremely important in Hawaiian culture. It is not unusual to this day for Hawaiians to know their ancestors going back for 200 years. Memory was a highly valued trait before the era of written language. Children would play memory games from a very early age. An individual with an excellent memory could thus find a valued role in the community. They would commonly recite an ali'i's ancestry going back over 20 generations. Status could be further increased by marrying well. Unlike many cultures in which such behavior would be condemned, the highest level of status could be achieved by marriage between two closely related individuals, if they were at the top rank, because the child would have greater mana (spiritual power) than either parent.

The highest level of ali'i were accorded the kapu moe, or prostration taboo, that required commoners to be fully prostrate in their presence. It was forbidden for commoners to look at them or to let their shadow fall upon an ali'i. These individuals were at the top of their hierarchy, with lower ranking ali'i making up their court, as dukes and duchesses in the European system of monarchy. High ranking chiefs were known as the ali'i nui, and whether male or female, this person wielded considerable power. The presence of the ali'i nui allowed for critical decision making even when chiefs were off at battle, or less commonly, when chiefs were killed. Upon the death of Kamehameha I in 1819 his favorite wife, Ka'ahumanu, became the first kuhina nui, a rank similar to prime minister. Her influence was so great she shared executive power with the succeeding monarchs until her death in 1832.

The Hawaiian aristocracy had all the trappings of a royal class. The distinctive feather capes, which reached to the ground in the highest ranking individuals, were created from the bright red and yellow feathers of hundreds of thousands of birds, which were sometimes released after the prized feathers were removed. Feathers were also used to create the arching woven helmets and the tall kāhili, a royal staff that preceded the ali'i wherever they went. Commoners were thus warned of the approaching royalty, and could either prostrate themselves on the ground or vacate the area.

Sections of land were called ahupua'a - ahu meaning a rock cairn and pua'a meaning pig - for the offerings, often pig, that would have been placed at the boundary for the local ali'i during the Makahiki season. It consisted of a piece of land that extended from the ocean to the uplands. Boundaries were often defined by physical features such as streams. Each unit would have a chief and a minor ali'i, konohiki, who administered the land. As they had at their disposal the variety of resources located at various elevations above sea level, they were relatively self sufficient and not highly dependent on trade. The lesser chiefs did not actually own these plots of land, but were granted their use in return for loyalty to the ali'i who controlled all of the land. Within an ahupua'a an 'ili contained special resources such as fishponds or cultivating grounds. A small family parcel was called a kuleana, a term that also means a responsibility.

Uhu ~ Parrot Fish

17

The ocean provided fish, shellfish, seaweed, salt and other necessities. Fish ponds were an interesting and unique use of coastal lands. This was one of the finest examples of aquaculture on the planet. Rock walls were built to enclose a small bay. Sections of the wall had small holes that allowed water, small fish fry, and invertebrates to enter. As these fish fed on the marine life in the pond they would grow too large to swim back through the holes and would be trapped. They also used the pond to store their surplus harvest of fish. If they caught more fish than could be readily consumed they would place the excess living fish in the pond. The fish could then be easily netted from the enclosure when needed.

Not surprisingly most of the permanent settlements were located in this coastal region. Middle elevations were best suited for the farming of various kinds of fruit trees and crops. From the uplands they harvested the large trees, such as Koa, that were essential for the construction of canoes. The Sandalwood trees that played such a vital role in lucrative post-contact trade in the early 1800's were also found at these higher elevations.

An interesting aspect of this system was the role of the commoners, the maka'āinana. These individuals were in no form slaves or property of the ali'i. They were free to move about at their will, though they would often occupy the same land for generations. While they were occupying a particular parcel of land a portion of their harvest would be shared with the local ali'i. This would usually take place during the Makahiki harvest season in the fall. They would also be available to pitch in to help with various construction projects, or other communal chores. As mentioned previously, the ali'i had absolute power. However, if they exercised this power in a ruthless or cruel fashion they risked alienating their subjects, who were free to take their allegiance elsewhere. This would force the ali'i into a certain degree of restraint. Ali'i who abused their subjects routinely would never rise to higher levels as they would be lacking a sufficient number of followers.

Each group of ali'i would also have their kāhuna. Although the title of kahuna is defined as a highly skilled master in one of many disciplines, it is used here to describe religious leaders. These priests were consulted by the leaders before any important decisions were made. Questions such as when to fish, go into battle, plant crops, etc. would need to be answered by the kāhuna before these projects were undertaken. Though serving as trusted advisors, they did not question the authority of the ali'i. The kāhuna carried on very long and complex ceremonies seeking a favorable intervention of the gods. Many of these ceremonies involved recitations of over an hour. This required a long and complex apprentice period before an individual could rise to this highly valued role.

The major gods of the Hawaiian religion played an important role in the rich and diverse mythology of Hawai'i. Lengthy volumes have been devoted to this topic. This will be an overview of the four major gods: Kāne is considered the major god, and creation stories are often centered around him. Lono is the god whose intercession is sought for fertile soils and a rich harvest. Kūkailimoku is the god of war and was the chief god of Kamehameha. The last of the four, Kanaloa, is considered the god of the sea. These gods are different

Pele Rising

from traditional gods in that they take on various characteristics in their different forms. For example, Kane-hekili is lightning. Ku-mokuhali'i is the god of the upland forest, where the large trees needed to construct the ocean-going canoes are found. He was therefore venerated by canoe builders.

There are a large number of minor gods. The most famous of these is Pelehonuamea, the deity of volcanoes. Inhabitants of the island of Hawai'i, her current home, still frequently make offerings to Pele. Her home is in Halema'uma'u Crater in Hawai'i Volcanoes National Park. It should be obvious that this was a nature-based religion. Hawaiians have always been very much in touch with the land or 'āina. Along with these universal gods, each family had their own ancestral spirit, called 'aumakua. They were often a fish, bird or other animal that had a particular significance to that family. The men of the family would make daily offerings to these spirits. Family members would make great efforts not to disturb their 'aumakua, whether it be a shark, sea cucumber, turtle, caterpillar, bird or other life form.

Heiau, or temples, were created to honor these deities. The size would vary from small platforms sometimes created from one rock, to elaborate structures that could take years to construct. These larger heiau were raised platforms created from large numbers of stones. They would be solid rather than just walls. It was not unusual for one to be 70 by 40 feet and 12 feet thick. It is said rocks were passed from great distances by people lined up in a long chain, in a bucket-brigade fashion. The top of these platforms often contained carved wooden representations of the gods, an offering tower, and a small hut where the leaders could gather. Heiau dedicated to Kūkailimoku, the war god, would require periodic human sacrifices. The offering of a high ranking ali'i would be considered the most powerful. The individual was not always killed at the temple. He might have already been killed in battle and was then brought to the heiau as an offering. There are a large number of heiau that are still standing. It is not unusual to see fresh offerings of flowers or fruit located in their towers.

A discussion of Hawaiian religion is not complete without a look at the kapu system. A kapu, or taboo, is a thing or behavior which is forbidden, or a person, place or thing which is set apart as sacred or cursed. One example is those things that were universally forbidden, like women eating with men, or commoners interacting with high ali'i. Another form was when a specific action was outlawed for a set period of time. An example of this type of kapu would be when fishermen were forbidden to fish for a specific species of fish for a period of time so that the fish could spawn. When Captain George Vancouver gave Kamehameha some cattle, a kapu was placed on them for over twenty years. The favorite surfing breaks of the ali'i could be kapu to commoners, as would the best canoe launch sites. Kapu were therefore the major means that the ali'i and priests used to maintain control over the commoners.

The breaking of a kapu could result in death. There was a traditional protocol for gaining a reprieve if a kapu was broken. If the offender could escape and make it to a place of refuge, or pu'uhonua, he could be granted a pardon by the kāhuna and return home with no fear. However, making it to one of these locations was anything but easy. Often the main access was from the ocean and there were dangerous reefs that made getting ashore a tricky proposition. Land access could be obstructed by a well guarded, tall rock wall. People were also able to gain safety in time of war in these secure havens. An excellent example of a place of refuge can be found today south of Kealakekua Bay on the Kona coast of the island of Hawai'i. Pu'uhonua o Hōnaunau National Historical Park is being restored to its original condition in the late 1700's.

The Hawaiian family system is the essential element of the social structure of the islands. The main configuration was an extended family, the 'ohana. As mentioned previously, these 'ohana would occupy a slice of the ahupua'a and would have houses in the highland rain forest, mid-elevation farmlands, and on the coast. Certain family members would live at a particular elevation and participate in whatever subsistence activities were located at that level, such as raising taro and bananas at a mid-elevation homestead. They would give their surplus produce to other 'ohana members. Coastal members would give surplus fish and seaweed to upper elevation family members. This was not really a barter system but more just sharing your bounty with the rest of your relatives.

Family members tended to spend more time at the coast for many reasons, so the largest house would be built near the ocean. Any members of the 'ohana, as well as guests, could sleep there. One half of this house was a raised sleeping platform. It was covered with a thick layer of mats for sleeping comfort. There was a well defined pattern of who slept next to whom. Wives would sleep next to their husbands. Children slept in the same area, but there was no roughhousing allowed. They had to go outside if they wanted to play.

Unlike contemporary housing customs, there were a large number of different structures, each with a specific function. Most were communal and could be used by all members of the 'ohana. The largest structure in a settlement would be the hale noa described above. Women of the family had a house called the hale pea where they would stay while they were menstruating. Men were not allowed to approach a woman during her menses. Men had their own house, called the mua, where women were not allowed. Men would eat in this structure as well as make the daily offerings to the family 'aumakua. There were other buildings where specific work could be carried out, such as a canoe building shed for men and mat weaving and tapa making structures for women.

Pounding Poi

Most of the cooking was done outdoors by the men. The preferred method for a large volume of food was cooking it underground in an imu. A bed of hot rocks would be arranged in a shallow pit and covered with smashed banana trunks. Food to be cooked was wrapped in ti leaves. There would be bundles of items including both vegetable and animal products arranged on the bed. A wrapped whole hog was often cooked in this manner. After layering with ti leaves the pit would then be covered over with soil and the contents left to steam for many hours. The many commercial lūʻau as well as large Hawaiian family gatherings still cook in this manner. During rainy weather there was a small hut that would be used specifically for cooking.

In early Hawaiʻi, marriage customs were often quite informal. Sometimes commoners would not even have a ceremony. People were well aware who was married to whom. Usually the union was one man and one woman. But a man could have more than one wife and a woman could have more than one husband. The first marriage partner would typically have more status than subsequent partners. However, if a first wife did not produce a child and a second wife did, then the second wife would have superior rank. Sexual customs were definitely more relaxed than was the case in Western culture. Hawaiians were more monogamous than the stories of the first missionaries would lead you to believe, however. The situation mentioned earlier of close blood relatives marrying was far less common than speculated. It would only be undertaken by aliʻi of the highest rank. These aliʻi almost always had additional husbands or wives, so few children would be produced by their relationship with their relative.

Dance, or hula, took on many forms in Hawaiʻi. Hula would be performed by both men and women. Some forms of hula were sacred while others were performed for entertainment of both the dancers and audience. Hula played an important role in passing down the oral history from one generation to the next. All hula movements represent a particular action or event and so by following the movements you can see a story told in a most beautiful fashion.

Hula Dancer

The early Hawaiians certainly had a fondness for sports. Many of these were water based activities such as swimming, surfing, and canoe racing. The swimming ability of these individuals was amazing. Both boys and girls could swim daily from an early age. They could commonly swim distances in excess of a mile. Since so much of their daily life centered around aquatic activities, skill in the water was more of a necessity than a luxury. It is not unusual today to see a group of Hawaiians swim out one-half mile, spear fish for several hours and then return with a nice catch that they speared from depths of up to 100 feet without the use of scuba gear. The breathtaking agility of Hawaiian surfers is well known. The ability to ride the waves is even more impressive when you see the heavy wooden boards that were used for hundreds of years before the invention of fiberglass. Skill with canoes in heavy surf was an essential survival skill as well as a sport to these maritime people. Today both surfing and canoe paddling are popular sports in Hawai'i and beyond, so the tradition continues.

Makahiki Competition

Many of the land based sports were related to skills needed in battle, such as wrestling and spear throwing. Sports were designed to test both the athlete's skill and strength. Moving large boulders is an example of the latter ability.

The major sporting time of the year was the fall harvest festival, the makahiki, in honor of the god Lono. During this three month festival there would be a cessation of all warfare. Rival 'ohana and ali'i rooted for their favorite athletes in a broad spectrum of both land based and aquatic sports. The winners of these competitions were local heroes and were accorded the status of valiant warriors. It was during a makahiki that Captain Cook, to whom we shall now turn, arrived in Hawai'i.

24

Chapter 3
Cook to Kamehameha

Captain James Cook was one of the most famous navigators ever to sail under the Union Jack. He had been exploring
in the South Pacific for many years before he ever saw Hawai'i.

Cook with a gathering of Hawaiians by John Webber

He had a far better knowledge of Polynesian culture and customs than any European of his time. Generally he was considered to be more humane and respectful of indigenous cultures
than other explorers in the late 1700's. He was no doubt pater-
nalistic by modern standards, but this was the era of going out
to civilize the "savages." Cook made three voyages to the South
Pacific. It is his third voyage with which we are concerned. He
had already visited the islands of central Polynesia, including
Tahiti. In late 1777 he headed north to once again pursue that
European dream of a Northwest Passage between the Atlantic
and Pacific Oceans. Cook was surprised when he came upon a
group of islands in the mid-Pacific. He sighted the island of
Hawai'i first, but the northeasterly trade winds pushed him
too far to the west to make a landfall. The same thing hap-
pened with succeeding islands until Cook finally ended up at

Kaua'i on the western end of the chain. Cook was seeking fresh water and provisions. With his knowledge of the Tahitian language he had little difficulty communicating with the many Hawaiians who paddled out to meet the ships.

He received a warm welcome and began trading for the needed provisions. He made an earnest attempt to keep all of his sailors on board, since he was aware that many of them were infected with syphilis, but was not successful in this attempt and a new disease was released in the islands. He was surprised to find that the natives were mainly interested in trading for iron objects. Since these were uncharted islands he wondered how they were aware of the existence of iron. This has led to speculations that perhaps the British were not the first explorers to reach Hawai'i. The re-provisioning went on without problems until some of the Hawaiians were caught stealing iron objects. The rate of theft increased until Cook felt it was time to continue his exploration. The two craft resumed their northerly direction in search of the Northwest Passage, but not before noting the location of the islands on their charts. Cook named the islands "The Sandwich Islands" after his friend and benefactor, the Earl of Sandwich.

After a summer and fall of fruitlessly searching in Alaska for the Northwest Passage, Cook's two ships, the Resolution and the Discovery, headed south. It was at this point that a number of accidental occurrences caused Cook to arrive in Kealakekua Bay in a manner that resulted in the natives perceiving him to be the god, Lono. As Cook neared Hawai'i he planned to make landfall on Maui. Unfavorable winds lead him to cross the channel to the island of Hawai'i. In his search for a good moorage he circled the island in a clockwise direction, ending up at Kealakekua Bay on the south Kona coast. He fulfilled three of the predictions for the return of Lono that had been prophesied by the kāhuna. First he arrived during the makahiki festival in honor of Lono. Second he approached from the south. And third his large multi-sailed square-rigger looked like the cloud on which Lono was predicted to arrive.

Cook was undoubtedly surprised by his newfound status when he came ashore. In typical fashion, however, he put his position to good use and received many of his provisions for free, without the usual bartering. After months at sea the crew was more than willing to take full advantage of this situation.

Cook did not attempt to keep his men on board on this arrival as it would have led to certain mutiny. Many local women stayed on the ships and sailors took up quarters on shore. With this welcome, Cook even set up an astronomical observatory on shore to gather data on the constellations. His artist, John Webber, filled sketch books that were later published to illustrate Cook's journals. Unfortunately, the British overstayed their welcome. After almost six weeks at the bay they had seriously depleted the resources of the region, and stealing was again becoming a major problem.

Cook then sailed north for Maui. A storm came up in the 'Alenuihāhā Channel, which is common, and the Resolution was demasted. With no options, Cook limped back to Kealakekua Bay for the necessary repairs. The Hawaiians were not happy about this turn of events and theft became a major problem from the outset. The situation was so tense that Cook fired his main cannons as a show of force. The scene became desperate when a group of natives stole a skiff during the night. Cook was outraged and dispatched a shore party, including himself, to take the ruling ali'i, Kalani'ōpu'u, hostage to use as ransom for the return of the skiff. All went well at first and the chief came along without resistance until his wife started screaming and pleaded with him not to go. When the chief refused to go with Cook, things rapidly deteriorated, with the British being forced back to the shore. One of the sailors fired a musket loaded with shot at a native in reed armor. The gun misfired and the pellets bounced harmlessly off the vest. This gave the natives renewed confidence and they attacked with clubs swinging. Cook was killed by repeated blows to the head, and his body was taken. The rest of the British retreated to their ship. The Hawaiians believed that a person could gain the power of an enemy by taking possession of his body. After much dickering the British were able to regain possession of parts of Cook's body. No one knows what became of the rest. A monument was established by the British Navy at the site of Cook's death. They still return to the site and perform a ceremony in honor of the most famous explorer of the Pacific.

The British left with Captain Charles Clerke in command to return to England. Captain George Vancouver, a veteran of Cook's voyage, led several return expeditions to Hawai'i. The British came to be well respected by the Hawaiians in succeeding years. This relationship is demonstrated by the fact that the Union Jack is located in the upper left hand corner of the Hawaiian flag.

Now that Hawai'i was on the charts it became a major re-provisioning port for European and American merchants and whalers doing business in the Pacific. A few foreigners, or haole, remained in the islands. Some became advisors to the ali'i in subsequent years. Others were idle beachcombers enjoying a carefree life.

One of the young Hawaiians who is thought to have been present at Cook's death was a rising ali'i named Kamehameha, the nephew of Kalani'ōpu'u. In the aftermath of the European "discovery" he rose to power, becoming the first Hawaiian to unite all of the islands under one rule. He was well versed in the arts of war and had the ability to envision how the technology of the foreigners could be used to his advantage.

On the eve of Kamahameha's birth, sometime between 1737 and 1758, it was prophesied that a male would be born who would overthrow the ruling chief. Like King Herod of biblical lore, Alapa'inui perceived the solution to this threat to be the elimination of all male babies born at the time. Kamehameha's mother, Keku'iapoiwa, who was a middle ranking ali'i, fled to the barren Kohala Coast of Hawai'i to give birth. The spot can be visited today above the powerful waves crashing to shore on the northernmost point of the island. Maui is visible across the channel on a clear day. The newborn was spirited away and relatives cared for the child in the uplands of North Kohala until the threat had passed. Kamehameha lived the life of an ali'i youth in the chiefly courts of Kona and Ka'u, spending countless hours in physical training as well as learning all of the protocols necessary to his position. It should be mentioned that Kamehameha was a massive man. From measurements taken of his cape, which still resides in the Bishop Museum in Honolulu, he was estimated to be almost seven feet tall and weighed over 300 pounds.

The main chief on the island of Hawai'i at the time of Cook's visit, Kalani'ōpu'u, died in 1782. His choice for succession was unusual, and proved to be a recipe for conflict. He named his son, Kiwala'ō, as his successor, but placed his nephew, Kame-hameha, in charge of war by bequeathing him the talisman of the war god, Kūkā'ilimoku. Since war was essential to the maintenance of power this created an immediate problem for his son. Was his father purposefully testing him? This would seem the case as it was unlikely that the two would share power. Avoiding immediate aggression, Kamehameha withdrew from the Kona region and established himself at Kawaihae near his ancestral home in Kohala. Kiwala'ō eventually attacked first and many ali'i defected from Kamehameha. The winner of the conflict remained unclear however as Kiwala'ō was killed in battle.

Kamehameha the Great

It was shortly after this that Kamehameha came in contact with two young Englishmen, John Young and Isaac Davis. Rather than kill these captives he put them to work for him. They showed him how to most effectively use his captured guns and cannon. Kamehameha had small cannons mounted on his double hulled war canoes. John Young became one of his most trusted advisors over the years. Young married a Hawaiian woman and built a fine New England style home near Kamehameha's compound at Kawaihae.

A young American who gained favor with Kamehameha was John Parker. Captain George Vancouver had presented Kamehameha with several cattle in the early 1790's. The king placed a kapu on these cattle and let them run free to multiply in the uplands of the island. With no natural predators the wild cattle increased their numbers to the point where they were trampling crops and generally terrorizing villagers. Kamehameha hired the young Parker, who had jumped ship, to bring the cattle under control. Through resourcefulness the former sailor was able to capture some of the cattle and eventually domesticate them. Many of the cattle were butchered, introducing a new meat to the Hawaiian diet. Parker was given a few acres as a reward and expanded his holdings considerably when he married one of Kamehameha's granddaughters. He brought over Mexican cowboys to train the Hawaiians in the arts of riding, roping, and other cattle handling skills. They came to be called paniolo from the word Español. Parker built his ranch into the dynasty that eventually ranked as the largest privately owned ranch in the United States.

At this time Kamehameha's ambitions turned from the island of Hawai'i to Maui. Both Maui and O'ahu were controlled by the chief, Kahekili. While Kahekili was away on O'ahu, Kamehameha attacked Maui. To avoid lengthy warfare the two declared a truce that both assumed would be temporary. Kamehameha returned to Hawai'i to consolidate his power there. His chief rival on the island was the Kona chief, Keōua, who attacked shortly after Kamehameha's return from Maui. Kamehameha repulsed the invasion. While returning home via Kīlauea there was an explosive volcanic eruption and Keōua lost many of his troops. Kamehameha and others took this as a sign that the volcano deity, Pelehonuamea, was opposed to Keōua, who was severely disheartened by the event.

Kamehameha next decided to build a large heiau to Kū, the god of war. This heiau, called Pu'ukoholā, is still standing in Kawaihae and is part of the National Park system. It is the site of numerous cultural and religious events by Hawaiians and other Polynesians. Some have said that Kamehameha built this impressive structure by creating a human chain almost 20 miles long. Rocks were passed from hand to hand to the kāhuna who oversaw their placement. Kamehameha invited Keōua to the dedication of this heiau. Since the heiau required a human sacrifice, and the higher ranking the person the better, Keōua should have seen what was coming. He might have been so disheartened by his last defeat that he just placed his fate in the hands of the gods. In any case, his canoes were attacked before they even came ashore and he became the sacrifice that gave mana, or power, to the heiau. Kamehameha's control of the island of Hawai'i was never again in doubt. From this base he could pursue his dream of unifying the Hawaiian islands.

Kahekili, the king of Maui and Oʻahu, then attacked Kamehameha. This was the first of a new style of warfare for Hawaiʻi. Both of the leaders possessed cannons and fought a major sea battle in the European style. After hours of shelling, the battle developed into a stalemate without a victor. Kamehameha's opportunity came when Kahekili died in 1794 and his sons fought one another for control of his territory. This played into Kamehameha's hands as he defeated his rivals one at a time. Perhaps the most famous battle of this campaign was the battle for control of Oʻahu. Kamehameha forced his opponents up Nuʻuanu Valley, in present day Honolulu, and backed them up to a 1,000 foot pali, or cliff, where many fell or leapt to their deaths rather than surrender.

At this point Kamehameha controlled all of the Hawaiian Islands except Kauaʻi, located over 70 miles from Oʻahu. The Kaʻieʻie Waho Channel is the largest stretch of open water between any of the main Hawaiian Islands. It is known for violent storms that spring up without warning. This gave the island a relative degree of isolation from the warfare that occupied the other islands. It was only a matter of time until Kamehameha made his move, which came in 1804. He launched a large armada, but a storm sank many of his ships, forcing a hasty retreat to Oʻahu. After another futile attempt halted by illness and weather, he came to an agreement with the ruling chief, Kaumualiʻi, making him the governor of Kauaʻi. Kaumualiʻi agreed to pay an annual tribute to Kamehameha and thus the unification of the islands was completed.

The following years saw a period of peace developing in the islands. The monarchy was now solidified and the aliʻi remained unified under Kamehameha's rule. He had wisely decided that from an administrative position it was effective to name a ranking aliʻi to the position of governor of each of the major islands. One of his first appointments was to place a young aliʻi named Boki as governor of Oʻahu. Along with his wife, Liliha, he was to serve three successive monarchs in this capacity. Interactions with the Europeans and Americans increased dramatically during this period, but Kamehameha's force of personality was able to keep them well under control. He died in 1819, probably in his seventies, on the eve of the most far reaching invasion of all.

Chapter 4
Missionaries & Whalers

It was the arrival of the Congregational missionaries in 1820 that set in place forces that were to ultimately reshape the future of Hawai'i. The period of foreign influence following Captain Cook's death had a profound effect upon future developments. The location of Hawai'i at the mid-point in the Pacific Ocean made it a natural site for re-provisioning ships of all countries wishing to become major players in the rapidly developing trade with Asia. British merchants were quick to see the possibilities of this new "discovery." They wasted no time convincing the ali'i to seek increased status in the owning and wearing of European clothing, furniture, and all manner of manufactured goods. Weapons of war such as cannons and muskets were in particular demand while the fight for domination of the islands continued. Kamehameha was proud of these new modern goods and the fad was embraced.

The first trade commodity to allow the ali'i to make these purchases was sandalwood. This highly prized wood could be sold in China for enormous profit by European and American traders. This very slow growing tree was found in the upper elevations of the islands. The ali'i forced their subjects to harvest the wood and carry it down the slopes for loading. This work was so undesirable that the workers pulled up any seedlings of the tree that they found to hasten its extinction. The chiefs were now constantly in debt as they acquired more and more European goods. The bonanza could not last and these trees drew near to extinction in less than 20 years. The main role that Americans played in this trade was that they owned many of the ships that were hauling cargo between China and Europe. This shipping boom developed a market for ship re-provisioning by the Hawaiians. This, rather than sandalwood, had a lasting effect on the long term growth of the economy. Ships would always need fresh water, food, and a place for their sailors to get some rest and relaxation.

Against this backdrop of an expanding economy the American missionaries arrived just six months after the death of Kamehameha. Liholiho, Kamehameha II, was the new king, although in fact Kamehameha's favorite wife, Ka'ahumanu, held great power. It was largely due to her influence and that of his mother, Keōpūolani, who was of the highest rank, that the long standing kapu system came to an end. The event that broke the system was when Liholiho was persuaded to eat with the women, one of the most strongly forbidden behaviors. Many Hawaiians were irate over this violation of tradition, but some powerful ali'i and kāhuna stood behind him. When it was seen that the gods did not intervene and punish them, Hawaiians saw little reason to uphold the other kapu. In a very short time the traditional system that had maintained order in the islands for almost a thousand years had been abandoned by a large percentage of the populace. According to some accounts, Hawai'i was rapidly approaching anarchy when the missionaries arrived. Their timing could not have been better.

Ka'ahumanu

On their arrival the missionaries from New England quickly established bases on the islands of Maui, Hawai'i, and O'ahu. The lack of clothing worn by the women and the relatively lax sexual mores shocked the missionaries and they were not reticent about expressing these feelings. Many viewed the Hawaiians as savages to be saved from the fires of hell. Consequently it should come as no surprise that their welcome was less than enthusiastic. The missionaries steadfastly maintained their traditional manner of clothing and food preferences, although these were clearly unsuited to their new environment. This only served to further alienate them from the natives. This rigidity was diametrically opposed to the laid back life style of the islanders. The one bright spot in attracting the islander's interest was the fact that many had wanted to learn to read and write since their introduction to Western cultures. The ali'i were particularly eager students. Literacy would be a great advantage in their business dealings with the Anglos. The missionaries considered the ability to read the Bible an essential element of Christianity and were eager to teach these skills to the Hawaiians. Thus knowledge of Jesus was interspersed with basic language fundamentals. The first converts were ali'i who quickly applied pressure on their subjects to join the church. The beliefs filled a void left when the traditional Hawaiian religious beliefs declined. Converts were required to take formal exams to prove their knowledge of both English and Christianity before they would be accepted into the church. By 1830 fully 30% of Hawaiians were undergoing formal training to pass these exams.

While the missionaries were grateful to the ali'i for their patronage, they questioned the somewhat arbitrary power of the monarchy. As Americans, they also felt compelled to spread the concept of democracy to the islands. Rather than pushing for an outright change of the government, which would have surely failed, they had to settle for just planting the seeds and waiting for them to grow. The success of the missions did not go unnoticed. More recruits from the States were summoned and by 1838 the number of missionaries had increased to 90. They established Punahou School as a college prep institution for their children. In later years the youth of the wealthy sugar planters and businessmen attended as well. Punahou remains a distinguished school to this day and prides itself on the number of graduates who enroll in Ivy League colleges. It also has the distinction of being the alma mater of Barack Obama, the 44th president of the United States of America.

The monopoly of the Congregationalists did not go unchallenged for long. In 1827 a group of Catholic missionaries arrived from France. They were not welcomed, and in fact were locked up under the pretense that they were French spies out

Saint Damien, 1889

to weaken British influence. The American missionaries played no small role in this subterfuge. The prisoners were not released until a French frigate aggressively sailed into Honolulu Harbor and fired a few rounds from its cannons. Undoubtedly the most famous Catholic priest in Hawai'i was the Belgian, Father Damien. He arrived at the leper colony on the Kalaupapa Peninsula on Moloka'i in 1873. He ministered to the lepers for 16 years, until he eventually succumbed to leprosy. The Roman Catholic Church canonized him as a saint in October of 2009.

Around the same time as the missionaries arrived another very different group of Americans became interested in Hawai'i. These were the whalers that were home based in Massachusetts. Whaling ships started arriving in Lahaina and Honolulu in 1819. By 1824 there were 100 ships using Hawai'i as both a re-provisioning center, and a repository where they could offload their catch and continue whaling rather than return to New England whaling ports.

Another function of a stop in port was the opportunity to allow the sailors to blow off some steam after being confined to tight ship's quarters for months on end. It was this recreational aspect that put the whalers on a collision course with the missionaries. Stories of sailors' fondness for rum are often not an exaggeration. The many grog shops lining the harbors of whaling ports were a true vexation to the teetotaling clerics. They tried without success to get them closed down. The profits from the sale of alcohol caused many a believer to look the other way. A unique cottage industry also sprang up in Hawai'i at this time. When the drunken sailors were thrown in jail it would be necessary for a consul to intercede with the ali'i to secure their release. The best of these consuls supposedly made over $150,000 a year under the table. It was just a cost of putting into port in Hawai'i.

The sailors also created another, far more serious problem, and that was the spread of sexually transmitted diseases to the island women. It was customary for young women to swim out to the ships entering port. They would exchange their favors (as they say) for clothing, perfume, cash or whatever else was available. In later periods these activities would be relegated to port side brothels as in most port towns. The missionaries pleaded with the ali'i to keep the women from swimming out to the ships, and after lengthy discussions the leaders agreed. This did not remove the temptation, however, as the women would meet the sailors in the bars and return with them to their ships. The ali'i then decided that the sailors could not spend the night in town and the women could not go to the ships. This edict was more than the seamen could tolerate and the skippers of several vessels protested the decision. In one of many disputes between Ka'ahumanu and Governor Boki, he sided with the whalers. She remained steadfast, however, and the girls stayed on shore. When the whalers protestations proved unsuccessful a particularly incensed skipper, aptly named "Mad Jack" Percival, proclaimed that this was a declaration of war. He landed with a large number of sailors with the intention of burning down the church to teach the missionaries not to interfere in his affairs. His party was met by a large contingent of Hawaiians. As previously mentioned, many of the Hawaiians were very large men and there could be no doubt of the outcome. The missionaries had won this round, but the conflict was far from resolved.

The whaling industry benefitted the economy of the Islands in a number of ways. Many young Hawaiians were hired by the ships as crew. They usually worked out well, as nautical skills were an integral part of their Polynesian heritage. Extracting and refining whale oil created an industry of its own. Processing the whalebone, most famous as the framework of women's corsets, spun off as another business enterprise. The merchants who both bought the oil and provided the supplies needed by the whalers started to grow into powerful financial trading companies. Whales in the immediate vicinity of Hawai'i were quickly depleted and the whole process of whaling proved to be extremely cyclical. However, most of the whales processed in Hawai'i were caught in the frigid waters of the North Pacific and Arctic Oceans. One out of every five years would be an economic disaster. It was hard to make accurate predictions at all times. Still the industry managed to grow. At its height in the 1850's over 500 ships per year were making regular stops in the islands. At the peak of the industry 19 whaling ships were owned by Hawaiian interests.

Early Honolulu Harbor scene

Whaling was not done in by over harvest, as many assume. The presence of oil discovered by Edwin Drake in Pennsylvania in the late 1850's, though barely noticed at the time, was the beginning of the gradual decline of the whaling industry and the end of American involvement in the industry. Kerosene lamps quickly reduced the demand for whale oil. One by one other whale-based products were replaced by cheaper synthetic substitutes.

Only the merchants and trading companies, who had begun to diversify years earlier, were able to remain financially viable after the crash of the whaling industry. They too might have gone under if it were not for the arrival of the industry that was to sustain Hawai'i for the next one hundred years - sugar.

Chapter 5
Sugar Industry

Sugar cane was one of the crops that Hawaiians traditionally took with them when they set off for new lands. So the cultivation of sugar was nothing new to Hawai'i. The first large scale commercial sugar plantation was started in 1835 on the Island of Kaua'i. This was a one-thousand acre plantation on land leased from the king. The cultivation of sugar cane underwent a dramatic transformation beginning in the 1850's. Ironically, the California gold rush of 1848 was one of the driv-

Kauikeaouli, Kamehameha III

ing factors for this new industry. It was quicker and cheaper to ship agricultural products, including sugar, from Hawai'i than the Eastern Seaboard of the United States at this time. The potential agricultural prowess of California was not yet a factor because, who wanted to be a farmer when there were such riches to be made as a prospector?

The first problem that was faced in creating a major agricultural presence in the islands was the lack of land. Almost all of the land in Hawai'i at this time was occupied by the ali'i, and few Hawaiians were interested in becoming large scale export farmers. The missionaries owned some small holdings that they had been granted over the years. The only other haole with land, such as John Parker who founded the huge cattle ranch on Hawai'i, had married into royal families. Pressure had been placed on the monarchy to sell land for many years, but it was steadfastly resisted. As previously mentioned, the monarchy owned all of the land, with ali'i only having historical use of the lands that they occupied.

This was all to change with the Mahele of 1848. From their first arrival Americans had been pressuring the monarchy to become more democratic. From the time of Kamehameha leases and simple use of land were granted to Westerners for service rendered to the kingdom. However, they were never given a title or deed to the land. The new constitution of 1840 had also loosened up restrictions on land use and leasing, but the ancient system of the monarchy possessing title was not changed until Kauikeaouli, Kamehameha III, issued the Mahele. Under this system one-third of the land, called crown lands, was retained by the monarchy. One-third would be available to the ali'i, and one-third would be available to commoners. With this ownership came the right to buy and sell the land. The ali'i had the opportunity to buy the land that they were already occupying under the old system. They could pay this tax by relinquishing some of their holdings back to the monarchy. They were free to do as they chose with their remaining land. Since the days of the sandalwood trade the ali'i often found themselves in debt and the opportunity to sell land was very tempting. Some of the more unscrupulous Westerners also used legal technicalities to cheat the Hawaiians out of their land.

The case with commoners was different. They had to fill out a few forms and pay a very reasonable tax called a kuleana to obtain title to a small three acre tract of land. It should be kept in mind that, with the long growing season and fertile soil, it was possible to grow enough food to feed a family in comfort on this amount of land. The goal of this policy was to make Hawai'i a land of small farmers. Unfortunately, few commoners went to the trouble of registering their land. In fact, many didn't have the money to pay the tax. It should be noted that, as with other indigenous people like Native American Indians, the concept of land ownership was foreign to their frame of reference. They used the land to meet their needs but had no interest in holding a deed to it.

Land was opened up for sale to foreigners in 1850. To the Westerners, with their quest for land ownership, this was a golden opportunity. Within a period of 30 years Westerners owned 80% of the private land, rendering the Hawaiians basically a landless people. This is part of the reason for the popularity of the present sovereignty movement. But that is another story to be told later in this book.

Many of the descendants of the American missionaries went into business. After the decline of the whaling industry they became active in supplying the machinery and general supplies that were needed by the sugar plantations. This naturally led to their involvement in the shipping industry. In an island nation the importance of shipping is paramount to any business activity. The raw sugar needed to be refined and Californian Claus Spreckels bought up a high percentage of the crop for refinement in his mills. In a short time he was even growing his own sugar on Maui. The missionary descendants soon became involved in banking so that they would have the financial resources to tie it all together. Poorly managed sugar plantations that fell into debt were taken over by these trading companies. Some plantations were even muscled out of business by high shipping rates and high interest loans. These holding companies would make money even in years when the sugar prices were down, which was not unusual. The most powerful of these companies came to be known as the "Big Five." The Big Five were Castle and Cooke, C. Brewer, Alexander and Baldwin, Theo Davies & Co., and American Factors (Am Fac). The 19th century headquarters of these giants of finance can still be visited in downtown Honolulu.

The Big Five were all linked together by intertwining boards of directors. This made them a virtual monopoly that could not be challenged. They were the primary force behind the Great Mahele and its main beneficiaries. Since they had long standing roots in the community they came to be the trusted advisors of the monarchy. The monarchs clearly needed counsel in dealing with business relations with outside interests. The members of the Big Five were only too willing to provide this service, which of course also served to give them the inside track in all business ventures.

A series of constitutions were drafted by the monarchy to deal with their changing relationships with both the commoners and foreign influences. Constant pressure was exerted to force the government in the direction of a representative democracy. A two-chamber legislature was formed that contained elements of both the British Parliament and the U.S. Congress. This was fitting as the influence of these two countries was the dominant outside pressure on the monarchy. Kamehameha I leaned strongly toward the British. His successors swayed to one direction then another, but the omnipresent influence of the missionaries and their descendants, who were largely educated in America, could leave little doubt as to which power would ultimately prevail.

A good example of American influence in the islands was the American Reciprocity Act of 1874. In return for allowing Hawaiian sugar to be imported duty free the United States got the use of Pearl Harbor as a naval base. This agreement gave Hawaiian sugar a very competitive price position in the States and gave the U.S. Navy perhaps the finest harbor facility in the Pacific Ocean. The ties were only to grow closer as commerce weaved the two countries into a complex trade network with financial benefits for both.

Let us now examine the labor needs of the sugar industry. Both sugar and pineapple, which began to be grown commercially in the late 1800's, are labor intensive crops. In addition to requiring intensive hand labor, both crops required physically demanding work in a hot climate. Needless to say, there were few people eager to take these jobs. As you would expect, the Hawaiian people were the first labor source to be tried. The Islanders did not like working in the cane fields and were accustomed to a more laid back lifestyle. They were able to feed and shelter themselves without working the regimented shifts required by the plantations.

The first outside labor force to be imported were Chinese coolies brought to the islands in 1852. They were hired directly from China on five year contracts. They were provided living quarters and limited food and clothing allowances. If they refused to work to the plantation owner's satisfaction, they would be jailed until they changed their attitude. Most of the Chinese did not enjoy plantation life and left the plantations as soon as their contracts were completed, returning to China with their savings. This capital would be sufficient to set them up very well in China. Others stayed on in the islands and moved into the cities where many went into business. In short order a Chinatown was forming in Honolulu, and in 1886, of all business licenses issued in Honolulu, 60% went to Chinese individuals. By the late 1800's the Chinese made up approximately one-fourth of the population of Honolulu. Some of these businesses did very well and the resources were available to stimulate other Chinese to go into business. Between 1852 and 1876 many thousands of Chinese immigrated to Hawai'i. By the time of annexation a total of over 45,000 Chinese had relocated to the islands.

By the mid 1860's the Chinese outnumbered Caucasians in Hawai'i. This was a source of worry to some of the Westerners who were generally very biased against the Chinese. Another problem with the contract labor system was that it too closely resembled slavery for the likes of some. As slavery was just being abolished in the States it was a topic of heated debates. The issue quickly became moot because of the Chinese Exclusion Act of 1882. Americans placed pressure on Hawaiians to honor this act if they wanted to retain duty free status on their sugar. The Hawaiian Kingdom passed its own exclusion act in 1888 in succumbing to this pressure. The cries of "yellow peril" created a kind of hysteria that was much more pronounced on the mainland than in Hawai'i, which was rapidly developing a multi-cultural character of its own. When the first individuals of Chinese ancestry were elected to the Territorial legislature in 1927, this multiculturalism was institutionalized. Hiram Fong, whose father was a Chinese field laborer, put himself through Harvard Law School. He was a court attorney who entered politics and was elected to the U.S. Senate after statehood, reflecting the degree of acceptance of individuals of various ethnic groups prevalent in the islands.

The first Japanese arrived in the islands in 1868, but it was almost 20 years later before widespread migration to Hawai'i from Japan took place. In 1886 the government of Japan, which was experiencing severe overcrowding, was instituting policies to encourage emigration to Hawai'i. The Eta, the lowest class of Japanese, were the focus of these policies. Few Japanese women moved to Hawai'i and the men had the goal of saving up $3,000 from their contracts and then returning to Japan. Eventually over 180,000 Japanese came to Hawai'i under the contract labor system. These workers were highly valued by the plantation owners because they were obedient, caused few problems, and were considered hard workers.

Early Sugar Workers

As the attitudes of the Japanese plantation workers started to change and they began to see the economic potential in remaining in Hawai'i rather than returning to Japan, many sent back to Japan for "mail order" brides. Though marriage to individuals not of Japanese ancestry was culturally discouraged, many began marrying individuals of different ethnicity which led to the rich cultural mix that composes Hawai'i at present. The second and third generations of Japanese workers were more integrated with Hawaiian society than their parents. Many entered business or set up small truck farms for growing fresh produce on completion of their contracts. Japanese language newspapers such as the *Hawaii Hochi* were started and attracted many loyal readers.

Most European laborers demanded higher wages and more say in their working conditions, making them unacceptable to the planters. Only the Portuguese were willing to work for lower wages because of rough economic times. Beginning in 1878, immigrants came to Hawai'i in considerable numbers from the islands of Medeira and the Azores, a place with similar terrain and climate. Since they were considered closer to the planters' own ethnic background than the Asians, the Portuguese were often put in the role of overseers, or luna, as they were called. Even working in the fields the Portuguese were paid higher salaries than Asians doing the same labor.

In the late 1880's another effort was made to bring larger numbers of Hawaiians into the sugar industry. Upon her death, Princess Bernice Pauahi Bishop's will created the Bishop Estate. She was the final heir to the Kamehameha dynasty and left thousands of acres of land, one-ninth of the land in Hawai'i, to her estate. The land was to be used to generate funds that would benefit Native Hawaiians. To carry out this mandate the Kamehameha School for boys was founded in 1887. The emphasis of the training was vocational agriculture. The girl's school opened in 1894 focusing on childcare and domestic work. The main goal was to train Hawaiian children to be good Christians and to Americanize them. The Board of Trustees of the estate was composed of haole, most well connected with the Big Five. It is an interesting side note that the first principal of the school, William Oleson, was one of the leaders of the revolution of 1893. In the early years of the school, alumni complained that they were being short changed by the narrow focus. As more and more graduates went on to college the vocational emphasis was abandoned. All in all the vocational programs at the Kamehameha Schools did not greatly increase the number of Hawaiians going into plantation work.

The last nationality of laborers to be brought over in large numbers from Asia to work the sugar fields were workers from the Philippines. By 1932 over 100,000 Filipinos had been brought in to work in the plantations. The sugar planters sought to keep the Asian immigrants from the various countries separate, encouraged disputes between these groups, and made efforts to keep them from unifying, which would have given the laborers more power. Some groups, such as the Filipinos, were even divided among themselves. Conflicts existed between Tagalog and Ilocano. One of the toughest challenges facing early labor organizers in the islands was getting the various ethnic groups to work together to reach their common goals. In a subsequent chapter the rise of organized labor in the twentieth century will be explored.

All of the individuals making up the Hawaiian labor force arrived in the islands speaking their own language or dialects. In order to be able to communicate, the universal language of pidgin evolved, with phrases from many languages. The native Hawaiians picked up pidgin along with their native language and it is still widely spoken on all of the islands by "locals" of all ethnicities.

Chapter 6
Hawaiian Monarchy

An examination of the Hawaiian government that was operating during the tumultuous changes of the 19th century will assist in understanding this era. Liholiho, who succeeded his father, Kamehameha, called himself Kamehameha II. It was shortly after Liholiho's succession that he put an end to the old gods. Impressed by the trappings of royalty, he cut quite a handsome figure in his English finery. His favorite wife, Princess Kamāmalu, was equally impressive in her ornate gowns and fine jewelry. Concerned about the impact of disease on the Hawaiians and seeing the need for greater law and order in the new society so heavily influenced by foreign contact, Liholiho decided to take a trip to England to meet King George III and seek his advice. Although the Hawaiian monarchs failed to inform the king of their intended visit and landed without fanfare in Portsmouth in the spring of 1824, they were courteously treated. While undergoing tutoring in the British social graces, first Kamāmalu and then Liholiho caught the measles. This disease, to which the Hawaiians had no natural immunity, often proved fatal in the islands. Even with the advanced medical practices of the British and the attendance of King George's personal physician, both died in the span of a few days. Before departing for England, Liholiho had designated his younger brother, Kauikeaouli, as the succesor and established Ka'ahumanu as Regent. The bodies of Liholiho and Kamāmalu were returned to their homeland by Lord Byron, cousin of the poet, aboard the H.M.S. *Blonde*.

Liholiho, Kamehameha II

Kauikeaouli, Kamehameha III, became king, but Ka'ahumanu retained extraordinary power. She and other ali'i had petitioned for membership in the church. Hiram Bingham, the minister of Kawaiahaʻo church in Honolulu, placed them on six months probation, but finally admitted them to membership. A large number of commoners quickly followed suit and in a short while Bingham was preaching to crowds of over a thousand. Kauikeaouli, unenthusiastic about church membership, set about undermining the Christians in earnest when Kaʻahumanu died in 1832. He lifted the penalties for adultery and slept with his sister, Nāhiʻenaʻena, following ancient tradition. He had already been a saloon keeper and supposedly forced some Christians to drink. He was a patron of the traditional Hawaiian arts including the hula, condemned by the missionaries as a heathen dance. All of these actions caused an uproar among the Christian aliʻi. They forced Kamehameha

Kawaiahaʻo Congregational Church

III to renounce these actions and return to the Christian values of Kaʻahumanu in 1835. He took this as a repudiation of his authority and abandoned caring about affairs of state. This allowed foreigners, particularly the missionaries, to greatly increase their power in the kingdom. Little changed in day to day morality, however, which led Mark Twain to state in the 1850's, "sin no longer flourishes here in name, only in reality."

Due to the influence of his haole counselors, Kauikeaouli issued the Declaration of Rights, which gave the foreigners a stronger legal foothold in the islands. Such inside pressure also led Kamehameha III to proclaim the Mahele, which gave foreigners a mechanism for owning land outright in the islands for the first time. Many who had acquired land through intermarriage with prominent aliʻi could now greatly expand their holdings by means of purchasing additional acreage.

It was during this period that the British, French, Russians, and Americans were all vying for influence over Hawai'i. A group of Americans pushed for annexation in the late 1840's. This first of many attempts was successfully resisted by Kauikeaouli, but a reciprocity treaty creating a most favored

nation status between the two countries was signed on December 20, 1849. Kamehameha III died in 1854 having overseen the erosion of Hawaiian sovereignty in terms of both domestic and international affairs during his reign, which was the longest of any Hawaiian monarch.

Alexander Liholiho, Kamehameha IV, a grandson of Kamehameha, had been adopted by his uncle, Kauikeaouli, following the traditional practice of hānai, where a child was given to be raised by another relative

Alexander Liholiho, Kamehameha IV

or family. He was an avid scholar and, while still a teenager, had traveled to the United States and Europe with his brother, Lot Kapuāiwa, under the tutelage of Dr. Gerrit Judd.

As a side note, Dr. Judd, who arrived in the islands as a medical missionary, was probably the most influential and trusted advisor of the monarchy. He held the position of Prime Minister for many years as well as serving as financial manager for several kings.

Kamehameha IV and his wife, Emma, were great admirers of all things British. When a son was born to the royal couple they named him Albert Edward, after the son of Queen Victoria. Tragically, Prince Albert died at age four, the last child born to any Hawaiian monarch. The greatest legacy left by the king and his queen was the establishment of The Queen's Hospital. They helped establish the Episcopal church and helped found what are now 'Iolani School and St. Andrew's Priory.

These pro-British actions played into the hands of some haole who wanted closer ties with America. They could again talk of a British threat to the independence of the islands. In actuality, the British had many opportunities to forge tighter bonds with Hawai'i and did not seem greatly interested. As with many of his predecessors, the king's health was never strong, and he died in 1863 at the young age of 29.

He was succeeded by his brother Lot Kapuāiwa, Kamehameha V. The last of the Kamehameha bloodline, he was a much more forceful ruler than his brother. He wished to

Lot Kapuāiwa, Kamehameha V

restore the power of the monarchy and set out to achieve this goal. Unconcerned with haole influence, Lot's immediate goal was to replace the Constitution of 1852 with a new constitution that would rein in the power of the foreigners, or at least slow down their drive for control. The Hawaiian Legislature during this time period was operating under a particularly unfavorable set of circumstances. Haole members refused to learn Hawaiian while Hawaiian members refused to speak English in the legislative chambers, although they were fluent. It is hard to imagine a less efficient way to run the government. Lot broke the stalemate by removing power from the legislature altogether and assuming complete control himself. He was, however, careful to create a political climate favorable to business interests. The sugar plantations started to import Asian workers under his reign and profits soared. He was

William Lunalilo

prudent in financial matters and made sure that the government was adequately funded. During his reign Hawai'i reached a favorable balance of trade for the first time in its history. By walking this delicate tightrope he was able to benefit both the monarchy and haole business interests. Like the four Hawaiian kings before him, Lot died young. A lifelong bachelor, he died on his 40th birthday in 1872.

With no clear successor the job of picking the next monarch passed to the legislature. The two leading contenders were David Kalākaua and Prince William Lunalilo, who was derisively called "Whiskey Bill" by his detractors. Lunalilo was a charming man who was beloved by Hawaiian commoners. He was elected and promptly appointed Americans to three of the four major cabinet positions. He was perceived to be more interested in a good party than in running the government and Hawaiian interests became further undermined. After less than two years in office his untimely death caused the process of succession to again fall to the legislature.

The main contenders were Queen Emma, Alexander Liholiho's wife, and again, David Kalākaua. This time Kalākaua

was victorious. This touched off riots by Emma's supporters and the British marines were called in to restore order. Eventually things quieted down and King Kalākaua was able to take up his role as monarch. By this time the haole sugar interests were exerting ever more governmental control, both directly and indirectly. Kalākaua saw this as a threat to his power and tried to exert more autonomy.

He was a great champion of Hawaiian arts in all of their forms. His patronage of the hula in particular was not to the liking of the Christian

King David Kalākaua

missionaries who had been trying to stamp out what they viewed as lewd dancing since their arrival in the islands. The resurrection of the hula and other traditional arts from near extinction, coupled with his well known love of drinking, gambling and entertaining resulted in his being dubbed the "Merry Monarch." In honor of Kalākaua's crusade to revive the Hawaiian's traditional dance, the most prestigious hula festival in the islands, Hilo's world-renowned Merrie Monarch Festival was named after him.

One of Kalākaua's projects for improving the status of the monarchy was the creation of a palace worthy of royalty in Honolulu. 'Iolani Palace, which still stands next to the Hawai'i State Capitol, was the end result of his efforts. The palace, which is the only palace on U.S. soil, has undergone a major renovation to restore it to its previous glory. The staff of the 'Iolani Palace Museum has sent out a worldwide appeal in search of Palace artifacts, resulting in the return of an array of regal objects. Many of the sugar planters saw the palace as an enormous waste of resources, but the Hawaiians clearly disagreed. Along with the trappings of royalty, the king traveled widely with his wife, Queen Kapi'olani, to spread knowledge of his kingdom. There were none of the clumsy attempts at social sophistication of earlier monarchs. King Kalākaua was a truly cosmopolitan man who traveled easily in the ranks of royalty. He was particularly well received in the United States, which he saw as the country most integrally involved in the future welfare of the Hawaiian Kingdom.

From the 1840's the power of the monarchy had been limited by a constitution of one form or another. These constitutions varied in both scope and power, depending on the nature of the monarch in power, and the relationship of the monarch with the moneyed interests who saw the constitutions as giving at least a measure of security to their Hawaiian investments. Kalākaua's luxurious taste dictated the necessity of maintaining a reasonable relationship with the moneyed interests. Against his better judgment he agreed to a new constitution in 1887 that transferred more power from the king to the legislature. Hawaiian resentment against this constitution, called the "Bayonet Constitution" for the force used to get the king to sign it, caused an escalation of tension that would come to a head under the next monarch. King Kalākaua died while on a trip to San Francisco in 1891. He was succeeded by his sister, Queen Lili'uokalani, the last of the Hawaiian monarchs.

Upon coming to power Lili'uokalani made the abolition of the 1887 constitution and restoration of power to the monarchy her major goals. She was far less willing to compromise than her brother had been. Her interests were diametrically opposed by a growing number of Americans who were interested in Hawai'i becoming a U.S. territory. She was overthrown in a largely bloodless revolution in 1893.

Chapter 7
Revolution

As the sugar companies became ever more powerful they became less and less willing to allow the power of the monarchy to remain unchecked. After rising to the throne at the age of 52, Queen Lili'uokalani moved quickly to revoke the constitution of 1887, which her brother had signed under duress. She was aware of the potential danger of eliminating this constitution, but underestimated the power of the sugar planters and merchants. She also wished to replace all of her haole ministers with Hawaiians.

A number of Americans in the islands found this threatening and thirteen of them, led by Lorrin Thurston, formed the Annexation Club. Many of the members of this club, including Thurston, became the nucleus of the Committee of Safety. While he was in Washington, Thurston set up a secret meeting with President Harrison. He was given verbal assurances that Harrison favored annexation. The Hawaiian legislature of 1892 was more chaotic than usual. The followers of the queen wanted a constitutional convention to draft a new constitution which would restore power to the royalty. The followers of Thurston, on the other hand, were pushing for a constitution that would speed the path to annexation. With all of this infighting, essential matters such as appropriation bills, were ignored. Queen Lili'uokalani backed a bill to create a national lottery as a revenue source, a measure that was far ahead of its time. A less enlightened bill that would have licensed and legalized opium was also proposed. Maintaining hopes of bankrupting the country and thus forcing annexation, the queen's adversaries opposed all revenue bills. The queen appointed her seventh cabinet of the year amid a storm of controversy.

A new constitution was then proposed by the queen. Two of its major features were that only Hawaiian subjects could vote, and property qualifications for voting would be removed. Lili'uokalani was well aware of the potential ramifications of this new constitution. She postponed announcing the new constitution as she feared that it could very well lead to a haole revolution.

News of the constitution was leaked and the Americans made their move. Thurston and his friends were convinced that the queen would soon ruin the country. The Committee of Safety was formed and they began drafting papers for a provisional government on January 15, 1893. The queen went

Lorrin A. Thurston

to the American Minister, John Stevens, to see if he would back the monarchy, but he had been meeting secretly with the conspirators and would give her no assurances. Several hundred supporters of the queen gathered in the Palace Square to voice their support. A crowd of 1,500 gathered to hear what the Committee of Safety had to say. Tensions remained high and the following Monday four boatloads of troops from the U.S.*Boston* entered Honolulu under orders from Stevens. Sanford Dole, head of the Supreme Court, became president of the provisional government. The Committee of Safety then took possession of the government buildings and the new government was recognized by Minister Stevens. Queen Lili'uokalani, wishing to avoid bloodshed, surrendered under protest to the United States and the revolution was accomplished.

The annexationists, including Thurston, traveled to Washington to ask for territorial status, but the administration had changed and Grover Cleveland, a democrat, was now president. Cleveland put them on hold and sent his own delegate to Hawai'i to research the revolution. John Blount, a former Congressman, was wined and dined by the Big Five. They assumed that he would naturally take their side, but he gathered over 1,000 pages of testimony from a broad cross section of Hawaiians. He urged Cleveland not to sign the annexation treaty and to reject the claims of Thurston and his allies that they represented the people of Hawai'i.

Based on a careful assessment of Blount's report Cleveland made a speech to Congress on December 18, 1893. Here are some excerpts from that speech.

To the Senate and House of Representatives:
"As I apprehend the situation, we are brought face to face with the following conditions:

The lawful Government of Hawai'i was overthrown without the drawing of a sword or the firing of a shot by a process every step of which, it may be safely asserted, is directly traceable to and dependent for its success upon the agency of the United States acting through its diplomatic and naval representatives.

But for the notorious predilections of the United States Minister for annexation, the Committee of Safety, which should be called the Committee of Annexation, would never have existed.

But for the landing of the United States forces upon false pretexts respecting the danger to life and property the committee would never have exposed themselves to the pains and penalties of treason by undertaking the subversion of the Queen's Government.

But for the presence of the United States forces in the immediate vicinity and in position to afford all needed protection and support the committee would not have proclaimed the provisional government from the steps of the Government building.

And finally, but for the lawless occupation of Honolulu under false pretexts by the United States forces, and but for Minister Stevens' recognition of the provisional government when the United States forces were its sole support and constituted its only military strength, the Queen and her Government would never have yielded to the provisional government, even for a time and for the sole purpose of submitting her case to the enlightened justice of the United States.

Believing, therefore, that the United States could not, under the circumstances disclosed, annex the islands without justly incurring the imputation of acquiring them by unjustifiable methods, I shall not again submit the treaty of annexation to the Senate for its consideration, and in the instructions to Minister Willis, a copy of which accompanies this message, I have directed him to so inform the provisional government.

But in the present instance our duty does not, in my opinion, end with refusing to consummate this questionable transaction. It has been the boast of our government that it seeks to do justice in all things without regard to the strength or weakness of those with whom it deals. I mistake the American people if they favor the odious doctrine that there is no such thing as international morality, that there is one law for a strong nation and another for a weak one, and that even by indirection a strong power may with impunity despoil a weak one of its territory.

By an act of war, committed with the participation of a diplomatic representative of the United States and without authority of Congress, the Government of a feeble but friendly and confiding people has been overthrown. A substantial wrong has thus been done which a due regard for our national character as well as the rights of the injured people requires we should endeavor to repair. The provisional government has not assumed a republican or other constitutional form, but has remained a mere executive council or oligarchy, set up without the assent of the people. It has not sought to find a permanent basis of popular support and has given no evidence of an intention to do so. Indeed, the representatives of that government assert that the people of Hawai'i are unfit for popular government and frankly avow that they can be best ruled by arbitrary or despotic power.

The law of nations is founded upon reason and justice, and the rules of conduct governing individual relations between citizens or subjects of a civilized state are equally applicable as between enlightened nations.

These principles apply to the present case with irresistible force when the special conditions of the Queen's surrender of her sovereignty are recalled. She surrendered not to the provisional government, but to the United States. She surrendered not absolutely and permanently, but temporarily and conditionally until such time as the facts could be considered by the United States. Furthermore, the provisional government acquiesced in her surrender in that manner and on those terms, not only by tacit consent, but through the positive acts of some members of that government who urged her peaceable submission, not merely to avoid bloodshed, but because she could place implicit reliance upon the justice of the United States, and that the whole subject would be finally considered at Washington.

Actuated by these desires and purposes, and not unmindful of the inherent perplexities of the situation nor of the limitations upon my power, I instructed Minister Willis to advise the Queen and her supporters of my desire to aid in the restoration of the status existing before the lawless landing of the United States forces at Honolulu on the 16th of January last, if such restoration could be effected upon terms providing for clemency as *well as justice to all parties concerned.*

In commending this subject to the extended powers and wide discretion of the Congress, I desire to add the assurance that I shall be much gratified to cooperate in any legislative plan which may be devised for the solution of the problem before us which is consistent with American honor, integrity, and morality."

GROVER CLEVELAND
Executive Mansion,
Washington, December 18, 1893 1.

Queen Lili'uokalani, the last monarch of Hawai'i

The provisional government failed to heed President Cleveland's demands. Since their end run for annexation was foiled, they created the Republic of Hawai'i. Their strategy was

1. *http://info@Hawai'i-nation.org/cleveland.html*

to bide their time until Cleveland's term in office ended and they could again apply for annexation when an administration more favorable to their manipulations took office. They set up a constitutional convention to develop a new constitution for Hawai'i. The requirements for membership in the convention were simple: members must pledge support to the provisional government and resist all efforts to restore the monarchy. With this base of delegates there could be little doubt that the new republic would place the haole firmly in control. It came to pass that over two-thirds of the ministers in the new government were descendants of the Congregational missionaries who first landed 70 years earlier.

Native Hawaiians still held strong feelings of loyalty to the monarchy, and a plan was created to carry out a counter revolution in early 1895. This revolt, led by Robert Wilcox, a part Hawaiian educated in Italy, was doomed from the start. A few arms had been stockpiled by loyal Hawaiians and the Queen was drawing up a new constitution. Rumors of the plot caused the police force of the Republic to search in earnest for the weapons cache. On January 6 shots were exchanged between police and royalist sympathizers. The police prevailed and the short lived opposition quickly crumbled. Queen Lili'uokalani was implicated in the plot and placed under house arrest in 'Iolani Palace. She was eventually freed, after eight months of confinement, and went to Washington to plead her case, continuing her efforts over the ensuing years to no avail.

With the election of the Republican William McKinley as president in 1898, the annexationists felt the tide turning in their favor. The U.S. House and Senate continued their ongoing debate on annexation. Speedy military victories in the Spanish American War created an urge for territorial expansion and this could only have a positive impact on the annexationists. In early July both the House of Representatives and the Senate passed resolutions of annexation. On July 7, 1898, President McKinley signed the resolution. Hawai'i was now a territory of the United States. It has recently come to light that a petition was circulated at the time of annexation and the overwhelming majority of Hawaiians were in favor of the restoration of the monarchy. These Hawaiian royalists created the Home Rule party to run candidates for office under the Territorial framework of government.

Chapter 8
Territorial Days

With the arrival of territorial status U.S. laws were now the supreme law of the land. While the general American assumption exists that the democratic structure of government allows for a far greater degree of individual freedom than would be found under a monarchy, native Hawaiians did not share this view. The framework of government under territorial status is far different from that put in place when a region becomes a state. The Organic Act, passed in June of 1900, established the framework of the Territorial government, and broadened voting rights to include all male citizens, whether they were landowners or not.

Sanford B. Dole

There were three major sources of governmental power in the Territory of Hawai'i. The first pillar of power was the governor. This position was far different from the role of governor in a state. The governor was not elected by the people, but appointed by the U.S. President for a four year term. Sanford B. Dole, selected as territorial governor, had far more power than the governor of a state. He controlled all appointments to administrative positions, had absolute veto power over the legislature, could not be impeached, and had the authority to place Hawai'i or any part of Hawai'i under martial law at will. It is interesting to note that, even during Democratic administrations in Washington, a Republican or conservative Democrat served as governor until World War II. The interests of the Big Five were always well represented.

The second major source of power in the new territory was the delegate to the U.S. Congress. Representing the territory of Hawai'i, but unable to cast a vote, the delegate served to merely answer questions about the territory and provide interpretation about how a particular piece of legislation might affect Hawai'i. He further acted as a conduit for information to and from Hawai'i, holding meetings to inform islanders about relevant events in Washington, and carrying the concerns of Hawaiians back to Congress.

The delegate to Congress was elected by a majority vote of the citizens of Hawai'i. This was not as democratic as it superficially appeared. Citizens had to demonstrate literacy in the English language in order to be eligible to vote. This tactic, borrowed from the American South, was quite effective in disenfranchising a large number of Hawaiian residents. Furthermore, any candidates who did not have the blessing of the Big Five were not permitted to campaign on the plantations where a large number of Hawai'i's residents lived. The combination of these two factors assured that anyone with a point of view running counter to big business had a tough fight to be elected in Hawai'i. Despite these obstacles, the Home Rule party's candidate for delegate to Congress, Robert Wilcox, was victorious. His first act as delegate was to introduce a bill that would extend the land policies of the United States to the territory. This included homesteading provisions that the sugar planters found particularly objectionable. None of Wilcox's proposals were taken seriously by Congress and he quickly lost all effectiveness.

The second elected delegate to Congress was Prince Jonah Kūhiō. Ironically, he was an heir to the throne of Queen Lili'uokalani. He was convinced by Henry Baldwin, of Alexander and Baldwin, that by helping the Big Five he was insuring the economic future of the islands and therefore helping the Hawaiian people. With the support of the Big Five he won every election from 1902, when the Home Rule party was swept from office, until his death in 1922. Though Kūhiō represented the Republicans who put him in office there remained a tension between them. He typically won close to 90% of the haole vote when running, yet it was generally perceived that he genuinely cared about the plight of native Hawaiians.

The third source of power in territorial days was the Territorial Legislature. Members were elected by a vote of the people, but as with the vote for delegate to Congress, the franchise issue and plantation campaigning played to the advantage of candidates representing sugar interests. Though some pro-Hawaiian representatives were always elected, the Big Five maintained control of a majority of seats in the legislature. It would be accurate to state that the Republican party ruled the territory, much as the businessmen who overthrew Queen Lili'-uokalani had ruled between 1893 and 1898 during the days of the Republic of Hawai'i. This is all the more amazing when you consider the fact that two-thirds of the voters were native Hawaiians during the early days of the territory. The fruits of political power were not limited to the Big Five. Others with missionary roots in the islands, such as Walter Dillingham, made their fortunes on land development and other business ventures.

Prince Jonah Kūhiō Kalaniana'ole

It has been said that government was controlled from the lounge of the exclusive Pacific Club in Honolulu, where wealthy sugar planters met to plan their strategies for the future of the islands over snifters of brandy and Cuban cigars. The issue of race was never far beneath the surface. Though many of the planters had married into ali'i society in earlier days and therefore had offspring of mixed blood, they considered themselves the blue bloods of Hawai'i. In dealings with Washington they never missed the chance to state their position as the most pro U.S. element in the islands and hence the most stable and dependable. There can be no denying that the United States was a highly racist society at this point in its history, with the white race holding a virtual monopoly on power and status. Southern Senators in particular were fond of using the issue of race against the new territory. The multiethnic nature of the islands undoubtedly delayed the drive for statehood for many years. Against this backdrop it is easy to see why the planters, who maintained a permanent lobbying office in Washington, were able to wield such a disproportionate amount of power.

Labor disputes, resulting from poor working conditions, came under U.S. law with the passage of annexation in 1898. This gave the workers a certain, though limited, degree of autonomy that had previously been lacking. Five thousand Japanese plantation workers went on strike in 1909. The planters had been adroit at pitting one group of workers against another, so early strikes tended to be composed of workers of one nationality. At this time Japanese workers were being paid 25% less than Portuguese who were working the same number of hours per month. Strike breakers were hired at twice the rate of pay of the Japanese strikers. The strikers were evicted from their plantation homes. This early strike was a failure and the strikers eventually returned to work at their previous wages. Another strike by Japanese workers in 1920 ended with much the same result.

The Filipino Federation of Labor, under its fiery leader, Pablo Manlapit, went on strike at the same time as the second Japanese strike. They refused to coordinate their strikes and met with similar results. Though wages did not increase, working conditions were upgraded. Manlapit led a second strike of

3,000 Filipino workers in 1924. This time the strike was much less peaceful. The Filipinos were armed and attacked the strike breakers. The situation escalated into a full blown riot; sixteen strikers and four policemen were killed. Eventually the national guard was called in. The strike had again failed and Manlapit was expelled from the country.

The National Labor Relations Act was passed in 1935 as part of FDR's New Deal. This piece of legislation guaranteed workers the right to organize and to use collective bargaining to better their wages and working conditions. The courts upheld the constitutionality of the NLRA in 1937, which set the stage for its implementation. A strike in 1937 by Filipino workers finally succeeded and strikers received a 15% pay increase. By this time two-thirds of plantation workers were Filipino, so the effect of the strike was widespread.

The ILWU - International Longshoremen and Warehousemen's Union came to power in 1938. They led a strike against the Matson Line. The Matson Line was the shipping arm of

Early longshoremen in Hawai'i

the Big Five and had a virtual monopoly on all goods coming into and out of Hawai'i. A strike against them had the potential of bringing all trade in the islands to a standstill. The stakes were high and tensions quickly erupted. In Hilo, on the island of Hawai'i, the second largest city in Hawai'i, violence flared between strikers, strikebreakers, and the police. Fifty of the strikers were wounded in the ensuing gunfire. Although there were no deaths, the incident was called the "Hilo Massacre." The strike ended as a stalemate and the workers returned to their jobs with no appreciable gains. Despite this setback the ILWU had established itself as a major player in Hawai'i. At around this time the ILWU affiliated with the CIO - Congress of Industrial Organizations. The larger AFL - American Federation of Labor had also made a bid. Due to the fact that the AFL at this point in its history was considered a decidedly pro-white union the CIO won out. Organizing workers in the Islands would have been very difficult if the parent union was perceived as racist.

During World War II, which will be covered in detail in the next chapter, labor disputes were non-existent, as any stoppage of production was viewed as aiding the enemy. This situation was even more dramatic in Hawai'i, which was under martial law from the time of the attack at Pearl Harbor until the conclusion of the war. Wages were frozen in the islands by the military commander. However, union members were very proud of the role that they played in helping to win the war.

Shortly after the end of the war, in 1945, the ILWU won its bid to organize the plantation workers. They wasted no time in flexing their collective muscle. In September of 1946, plantation workers numbering 21,000 went out on strike. The sugar companies could not withstand this amount of pressure and Castle & Cooke was the first of the Big Five to settle. It was a clear union victory.

Jack Hall, a very colorful figure with distinct leftist leanings, became head of the ILWU in Hawai'i in the mid 40's. He was instrumental in coordinating a second strike against the Matson Line in 1949. Two thousand dock workers walked off the job and nothing entered or left the islands for six months. The strikers again won and the power of labor was clearly established. In his personal life things did not go so smoothly. Hall was called up in front of the Senate Committee on Internal Security. This committee was the Senate version of McCarthy's "red hunting" House Committee on Un-American Activities. As with many of his contemporaries he pleaded the 5th Amendment. At the time this was seen as an admission of guilt and he was arrested and tried on charges under the Smith Act. This act dealt with charges of teaching the overthrow of the United States government using force and violence. Though he was eventually cleared and never abandoned by loyal union members, it created a blot on his reputation that he never fully overcame. It should be admitted that many labor leaders in Hawai'i flirted with communism during the 30's and 40's. They were pushing for increased rights for workers and minority members, however, and were in no way involved in plots to overthrow the government of the United States or to ally themselves with the government of the USSR.

Hall's power within the union remained unchallenged and in 1958 he led another strike of sugar workers. The union again won concessions from the planters, setting the stage for a period of relative cooperation between unions and management, since the planters were forced to recognize that they no longer maintained sole control. It would also be fair to speculate that the better standards of working conditions and wages that the plantation workers won in the second half of the 20th century played a role in the massive closure of sugar and pineapple operations that took place during the 1990's. By 1998 there was not a single active sugar mill on the island of Hawai'i. Dole abandoned Lāna'i for cheaper production costs in South East Asia. The remaining sugar and pineapple operations mainly cater to tourists who have an interest in observing the former mainstay of the Hawaiian economy.

Pineapple Pickers

Chapter 9
World War II

You are well aware that the United States entered the Second World War with the bombing of Pearl Harbor on December 7, 1941. However, you may not be aware of the long term effects of that attack on the Hawaiian Islands. The attack was not as much of a surprise as we have been led to believe. The military was well aware of the fact that Hawai'i was a prime

Honolulu Star-Bulletin 1st EXTRA

WAR !

(Associated Press by Transpacific Telephone)

SAN FRANCISCO, Dec. 7.—President Roosevelt announced this morning that Japanese planes had attacked Manila and Pearl Harbor.

OAHU BOMBED BY JAPANESE PLANES

target of the Japanese as they expanded their empire in the Pacific. There was a high degree of military preparedness in general in the islands that included close surveillance of any Americans of Japanese ancestry whose loyalty could be considered suspect.

One of the new technologies being developed as the U.S. moved ever closer to war was radar. Both permanent and mobile radar stations had been set up in Hawai'i in anticipation of an air attack. However, the technology was not perfected and was considered somewhat unreliable by some in the military. At 7 a.m. on that Sunday morning two privates manning one of the mobile stations picked up a large concentration of aircraft. Neither man had previously seen this large a number of planes. The planes were incoming approximately 140 miles northwest of the islands. When the planes reached 120 miles out they called in a warning. The switchboard operator had difficulty locating an officer to respond to the privates. When an officer was eventually located he stated that either the planes were on maneuvers from Hickam Air Base on O'ahu or they were a large flight of inbound B-17s from the mainland. The later supposition is hard to take seriously as the planes were approaching from the west.

The Japanese could not have picked a more opportune time to attack. After a long Saturday night of partying in Honolulu many of the troops would not have been at their sharpest on an early Sunday morning. The Japanese planes reached their primary target of Pearl Harbor at five minutes before 8 a.m. Secondary targets at Hickam Field and the Army post, Schofield Barracks, also quickly came under attack. The warnings of the radar operators and the 4 a.m. sighting of a periscope by a mine sweeper off Pearl Harbor had both been ignored and the U.S. forces were caught by surprise. The results of the attack are well documented: 3,435 U.S. casualties, eight battleships and ten other large ships severely damaged, and 188 planes destroyed. The Japanese lost 29 planes and five midget subs that had been trying to blockade the entrance of the harbor to prevent the U.S. ships from escaping. It was an extreme bit of luck that all of the U.S. aircraft carriers were at sea at the time of the attack. These same carriers later were able to win a major naval battle when the Japanese navy was dealt a blow from which they never recovered off Midway Island at the far western end of the Hawaiian Archipelago.

The immediate effect of the attack on Pearl Harbor was rapid preparations for a land invasion by the Japanese. Many thought that the air attack was a precursor for a land assault on the islands within a few days. General Short ordered Governor Poindexter to declare martial law. The Governor called the president who had appointed him, FDR, to get his advice. Roosevelt agreed that he should comply with the order. He further stated that martial law would be short lived if there was no invasion. This turned out to be extremely inaccurate, as martial law remained in effect for the duration of the war, long after there was any real threat to Hawai'i. Poindexter was replaced by a military governor and the civilian government was stripped of all power. The military wielded enormous power during this period. They censored the press, froze wages and set the hours of work, controlled rents, regulated restaurants and bars, declared curfews and blackouts, and replaced the local courts with military tribunals with no writ of *habeas corpus*. These acts were blatant violations of the rights of Hawaiian citizens, but to criticize these measures was considered unpatriotic. The powerful sugar planters wasted no time in inviting high ranking military officers to their social events. In a short period of time the Big Five insured that they would be serving as advisors to the military, reinforcing their influence over the islands.

One of the first problems facing the military government was what to do about the 160,000 individuals of Japanese ancestry living in Hawai'i. This was a much more complex issue than measures that were taken to deal with Japanese Americans on the West Coast of the United States. In the first place there was no facility that could possibly be used to confine even one-third of these people in the islands. With the setback that the navy suffered at Pearl Harbor, neither the ships nor time required to move large numbers of people to the mainland could be spared. Furthermore, many Japanese Americans provided labor that was highly skilled and considered essential to the economic well-being of the islands.

Most of these Japanese Americans were patriotic citizens. The only group of Japanese in Hawai'i with mixed patriotism were the first generation of Japanese, referred to as issei, who had migrated to Hawai'i. A small group of the older issei men had sympathy with Japan, though they would never admit it publicly. The second generation, called nisei, were very patriotic Americans, often refusing to even speak Japanese with their parents. They would not wear Japanese clothing and asked their mothers to burn their kimonos. They also asked their parents to remove Japanese shrines from their gardens and homes. In denying their heritage they searched for a niche in this new society. These young nisei went down to the recruiting office to sign up in large numbers shortly after the attack on Pearl Harbor. Not only would the recruiters not ac-

66

cept their applications, but the nisei currently enrolled in ROTC programs were dismissed from these positions as well. Japanese Americans who were already members of the National Guard could not legally be dismissed. The military, however, wanted them off the islands as soon as possible. They did not want them present if there was a Japanese invasion. These individuals were shipped out to Wisconsin and reorganized as the 100th Infantry.

In January of 1943, the nisei were finally allowed to enlist. A new battalion, the 442nd Infantry, was created. These young men knew that they would only be allowed to fight in the European theater. The turn out was tremendous. Four thousand volunteered during the first week and nine thousand had enrolled within a month. Three thousand of these applicants were selected for membership in the 442nd. The 100th, like the 442nd, was destined to fight only against the Germans and Italians. They were finally given a combat assignment in 1943 and were sent to join the North African campaign, just as the tide was turning against the famous German, General Erwin Rommel. They played a major role in the invasion of Italy which shortly followed. They were involved in heavy fighting to capture Rome after German troops were sent to reinforce the rapidly failing Italian army. At this juncture they were joined by the 442nd. The two units fought against very heavy odds in the Northern Italian campaign where the Germans had determined to draw the line. They suffered casualty rates that were three times higher than the army average. The soldiers fought valiantly and ended up the two most decorated units in the history of the U.S. Army. They returned to Hawai'i as heroes and became some of the key players in a political revolution that has influenced the government of Hawai'i to the present day.

Members of the famous 442nd Regimental Combat Team in 1943.
Courtesy of Hawaii Japanese Center

Chapter 10
Statehood

The political power of the Big Five was not able to withstand the winds of change that were blowing through Hawai'i following the conclusion of the Second World War. Like African-American war heroes returning from the war who pushed the civil rights movement into high gear when they refused to accept their former roles, the returning Hawai'i soldiers were no longer willing to settle for second class citizenship.

Senator Daniel Inouye

Like veterans throughout the United States, many of the returning nisei went to college on the GI Bill. The fields of law, medicine, and teaching were particularly attractive to the Hawai'i veterans. A young man of great ambition, who came to represent the hopes and dreams of the returning nisei was Daniel Inouye. He had lost his arm in the fighting in Europe, putting an end to his dream of becoming a surgeon. He returned home with a chest full of medals, a true hero. After the war he received his law degree from George Washington University and returned to Hawai'i, where he became a key player in the evolving political scene. He was elected to the territorial House of Representatives and became the majority leader when the Democrats swept to power in 1955. Inouye was the first Japanese American to be elected to the U.S. House of Representatives in 1959, when Hawai'i had its first election after statehood. Elected to the U.S. Senate in 1962 he rose rapidly to a position of power. He eventually attained the powerful position of head of the Senate Appropriations Committee. At the time of his death in 2012 he was the longest serving member of the U.S. Senate and third in presidential line of succesion. After laying in state at the United States Capitol rotunda in Washington, D.C., Senator Inouye returned home to Hawai'i where he was buried with honors at the National Memorial Cemetary of the Pacific at Punchbowl. Governor Neil Abercrombie appointed Lieutenant Governor Brian Schatz to serve out the remainder of Senator Inouye's term.

After WWII, two major players arose to fight for control of the Democratic party in Hawai'i. The first was Jack Hall, the head of the ILWU. The long history of organized labor's ties to the Democratic party would set Hall up as a natural key player as the party rose to power. His supposed links to the Communist party, though they garnered major headlines in Hawaiian newspapers, did little to dim his popularity. His opponent for control of the party was John A. "Jack" Burns. Burns came up through the ranks of the party over the years. He was a detective in the Honolulu police department and thus was no stranger to the less affluent population of O'ahu. His ties with "the street" were of great value to him throughout his political tenure. He was known as a champion of the common man, whereas Hall's base was almost exclusively in organized labor. Burns developed particularly strong ties within Honolulu's Chinese and Japanese districts. After the war he was the first to capitalize on the emerging political power of Americans of Chinese and Japanese ancestry. He took many of the young Japanese Americans seeking office, such as Daniel Inouye and Patsy Mink, under his wing and helped them to launch their careers. This created a loyal group of followers as he began his bid to gain control of the Democratic party. Burns and Hall both tried to gain control of the 1948 state Democratic Convention. Neither man was able to garner a majority of delegates but collectively they were able to unseat the "old guard" of the party. Both men were wise enough to recognize that nothing was to be gained by undermining the constituency of the other. A coalition was formed without a clear leader. However, at the 1952 convention Burns gained control, with the shifting support of organized labor, and Hall refocused his energies on labor concerns, remaining a strong behind-the-scenes player in Hawai'i politics for years to come.

The now unified Democratic party took on the Republicans who had held a virtual monopoly on governmental power in Hawai'i since annexation. The elections in 1954 were the turning point. Democrats won two-thirds of the seats in the House of the territorial legislature and almost as large a percentage in the Senate. They have held similar or larger majorities in almost every legislature up to the present day. It was during this same decade that the issue of statehood would finally be resolved. When Hawai'i was annexed in 1898 it was never assured future statehood. No offshore territory had ever been granted statehood. Some said that Hawai'i would challenge the "Western traditions" of the United States. Early in his political career, Strom Thurmond of South Carolina stated, "the U.S. is the maximum development of Western culture - at the opposite extreme is Eastern culture which is dominant in Hawai'i." He then quoted Kipling, "East is East and West is West, and never the twain shall meet." Some Southern congressmen stated that Hawai'i was populated by individuals of dubious ethnic stock. They surmised, and not incorrectly, that members of Congress from Hawai'i would be liberal, particularly in matters of racial affairs.

Hawai'i created a Statehood Commission to keep the push for statehood on the agenda in Washington. Some of the facts that they presented in the early 50's are as follows. Hawai'i paid more taxes to the U.S. government than nine existing states, yet had no voice in how the money was spent. The population at this time was half a million, which was more than four existing states. Hawai'i had a larger population than any territory except Oklahoma at the time of statehood. Nine out of ten residents of the Islands were citizens - to counter the Asian influence argument. Almost every major power group in Hawai'i was in favor of statehood. In 1940, during the first election in which Hawai'i's citizens voted on the issue, voters favored statehood by a margin of three to one. Some of those opposed to statehood were native Hawaiians who contended that the monarchy had been illegally overthrown and therefore they desired no closer links with the United States.

On the U.S. mainland a poll in 1946 showed that six out of ten were in favor of statehood for Hawai'i. By 1954 this majority had risen to 78%. Every Hawai'i delegate to the U.S. Congress since 1936 had introduced statehood resolutions. When

John A. "Jack" Burns was elected to Congress for the first time in 1948, the number one item on his agenda was statehood. He crafted and lobbied for countless statehood bills. As with many other issues, the admission of Hawai'i as a state took on partisan overtones. It was clear to Republicans in Congress that Hawai'i would tend to elect Democrats to Congress. It was a correct assumption, as almost every Hawai'i Senator and Representative in the House has been a Democrat during the 50 years since statehood. Indeed, the overwhelming success of the Democratic party in Hawai'i in the early 50's was a force which proved detrimental to the fight for statehood. Southern Democrats in both houses of Congress were prime opponents of statehood, for the same reason they had been opposed to annexation 60 years earlier. Any diehard segregationist was justified in opposing Hawai'i, as the Hawai'i delegation after statehood was one of the prime supporters of subsequent civil rights legislation in the 1960's. Hawai'i's Congressional delegation has become famous as being progressive on many social issues in addition to civil rights.

Governor John A. "Jack" Burns

In the second half of the 1950's a rivalry developed between Alaska and Hawai'i in a virtual race for statehood. There were several similarities between the two territories. Both were not connected directly to the contiguous 48 states, and both territories had large numbers of non-white residents. Delegations from both territories quickly realized that if the other territory were admitted to statehood first it would place increased pressure on Washington to admit the second. It was decided that Hawai'i would not stand in the way of Alaska's being first, and the two territories joined ranks and shared common lobbying strategies.

Under continued pressure Southern Democrats began to soften their position, and Hawai'i's strategic military position appealed to some mainland Republicans. The House of Representatives was the first to pass a Hawai'i statehood bill in February of 1959. The Senate quickly followed with a similar bill on March 11th. President Eisenhower, a longstanding supporter of statehood for Hawai'i, signed the legislation on March 18, 1959.

Now all that was needed was for the citizens of Hawai'i to ratify these congressional votes. A special election was held on June 27. Hawai'i voters ratified statehood by a margin of 17 to 1. The only precinct voting against statehood was the small island of Ni'ihau, which was composed entirely of native Hawaiians. Hawai'i became the 50th state on August 21, 1959 amid widespread celebration in the new Aloha State. The flag raised over the new state was unique in the fact that it had flown over Hawai'i as a kingdom, republic, territory and now a U.S. state. In 1816, Kamehameha had commissioned his own flag to avoid the conflict that resulted when he alternately flew the British Union Jack and the American flag over his residence. As a result, the current flag of Hawai'i was born, seemingly a hybrid of the two flags.

The new state's first order of business was the election of Hawai'i's delegation to Congress and the election of a governor. It surprised no one when Dan Inouye won Hawai'i's single seat in the House of Representatives. What surprised some was that Jack Burns did not run for the Senate, but decided to stay in Hawai'i and join the race for Governor. More surprising yet was his defeat by Republican William Quinn, a former territorial Governor. Burns was to get his vindication when he defeated Quinn in 1962 and served a total of three terms as Governor. Democrats controlled both houses of the state legislature and the office of governor for the next 40 years.

50th State's first governor, William F. Quinn

Chapter 11
Economic Restructuring

With the arrival of statehood, and the increased democratization of power in the islands when the the Big Five lost control, some were thrilled to proclaim the arrival of a "new Hawai'i." Others contended that the new coalition presided over by Governor Burns and his allies was no more democratic than the near feudal system that it had replaced. As in all political systems there was an element of "to the victors go the spoils." However, unlike the old system, the people had the ballot box as a mechanism to voice displeasure should the new system get too far out of line.

In 1969, on the tenth anniversary of statehood, Governor Burns created the Conference on the Year 2000 Committee to chart a long range plan for the next 30 years. One of the subjects being studied was race. A statistic that came out of the study was that Hawai'i had by far the highest percentage of interracial marriages in the United States, approaching 50%. This was used to reinforce the image of Hawai'i as a melting pot. Another hot topic was the displacement of native Hawaiians from the land, particularly on O'ahu and Maui. Young people in particular expressed a great deal of skepticism about the whole Year 2000 project. The concept of Aloha was brought into question. Was it just a tourism marketing tool or was there a real feeling of sharing and concern for others? All in all the committee raised more questions than it answered, but it was a rare study of democracy in action.

The major driving force in the new Hawai'i was the changing economy rather than the new political system. The decline of the sugar industry, followed shortly by reduced pineapple production, created an economic environment ripe for a new source of revenue. Luckily for the islands, tourism was expanding to more than make up for the lost income. The number of visitors to Hawai'i increased from 40,000 in 1950 to 175,000 by the time of statehood. The boom continued as numbers increased to 1.2 million by 1968. By 1970 this sector of the economy was contributing more than one billion dollars yearly, over four times the value of the combined income from all forms of agriculture. Economic problems in Asia led to a slow down in total tourism growth in the late 1990's. Despite the recession that began in 2008, the rate of growth in visitors has increased to over 8 million in 2012, the economic contribution of tourism rose to over $12 billion and the maximum potential is hard to guess.

Early Waikīkī and Diamond Head

Several factors accounted for the tremendous growth of tourism. Before the Second World War, tourists made their way to the islands on expensive cruises with the Matson Line. The line built the first hotels on Waikīkī Beach to create a destination resort for these travelers. With the growth of the airline industry tourism grew, but it was the development of large capacity, high speed jets that allowed the masses to escape to the tropics. Many GIs who had spent R&R time in Hawai'i during the war joined the first waves of tourists to return to the islands in large numbers. The increase in disposable income spurred by U.S. economic growth was also a contributing factor.

The tourist boom fueled a second boom, that of the construction industry. The infrastructure needed to support this volume of visitors was tremendous. Not only did hotels appear at an amazing rate in the former swamp that was Waikīkī, but resorts were built from scratch in regions not even accessible by road a few years previous to their development. In a state with a powerful and well established system of labor unions this insured a large number of good paying jobs. All of the support industries, from concrete plants to architecture firms, were carried along on this great wave of prosperity. The construction boom carried on in high gear until the slow down of the early 90's.

Hawai'i's growth was not limited to tourists. The resident population, drawn by the booming economy as well as the desire to escape winter, increased dramatically in the decades following statehood. The population was right at a half million in 1950, and nearly 650,000 by statehood. By the early 1990's this population had doubled, but growth has slowed since that juncture. Projections put the population approaching two million by 2020.

The demand for land on which to build this myriad of new tropical oases led to the real estate boom that has also been a major contributing factor to the economy. Unfortunately, this boom has put home ownership out of reach for large numbers of Hawai'i residents. In an island environment the amount of land is physically limited in ways that mainlanders have difficulty comprehending. Land prices are necessarily very high in proportion to its scarcity. Of the 64% of Hawai'i's land that is privately owned, a high percentage is held by a small number of investors such as Kamehameha Schools (Bishop Estate). This places even greater restrictions on the amount of land that is available for sale at any given time. With the limited number of landowners, development has mainly been undertaken by hui. This is a Hawaiian term for a group of investors. Many of the hui that developed in the decades after statehood were controlled by individuals of Chinese ancestry. By withholding land from development the prices could be raised to even higher levels. This has created an environment in which many descendants of the original Hawaiian inhabitants of the islands are unable to buy land in their own homeland.

The red hot Japanese economy in the early 90's created a massive inflow of yen that drove land prices, particularly in the Honolulu area, to astronomical levels. A simple three bed-room tract house could be valued at one-third of a million dol-lars. While the market has slowed down dramatically since that period, land will never be inexpensive in paradise.

The geographic location of Hawai'i in the middle of the Pacific basin has always played a major role in the economy of the region. This Asian link has been further developed by the creation of the East-West Center, developed in affiliation with the University of Hawai'i at Mānoa in Honolulu. The center was established in 1960 to provide an academic think tank to examine the potential relationship between Hawai'i and the Pacific Rim. The recent decline in the value of the yen and the general slowdown of the Asian economic tigers has decreased Asian investment in Hawai'i, but the strategic location of the islands and the muli-cultural makeup of the population cre-ates a natural environment for economic partnerships between Asia and this westernmost state in the United States.

With the withdrawal of most sugar and pineapple planta-tions from the islands much agricultural land has been opened up for alternative uses. The last sugar mill on the island of Hawai'i closed in the late 1990's and Dole Pineapple elimi-nated their agricultural operations from the island of Lāna'i in the 90's as well. Since Dole controlled the entire island, it cre-ated the opportunity to redesign the island for alternative uses. This has lead to an increase in what is termed diversified agri-culture. Some of the major crops that are currently being grown for export are papaya, macadamia nuts, and coffee. All three of these crops have increased dramatically in the last ten years. Kona coffee, which is grown at mid-elevations on the leeward coast of the island of Hawai'i, is considered one of the finest coffees in the world. Papayas from the Puna region on the wind-ward coast of Hawai'i Island are now finding international markets. Macadamia nuts from Hilo are replacing pineapple in many suitcases as the food gift of choice for friends over-seas. Floriculture has emerged as another major agricultural focus of the islands. The orchids, anthuriums, gingers, and other cut flowers produced in Hawai'i are exported around the globe. The growing of produce for consumption in the is-lands is also increasing. Taro, the crop grown by Kamehameha himself in Waipi'o Valley, continues to be a common component of the Hawai'i diet, in the form of poi.

The newest forest product to be grown on old sugar land is eucalyptus trees. These fast growing trees are being marketed as a source of pulp for paper production in Japan. Tropical hardwoods such as koa and 'ōhia are being replanted on upland slopes of Hawai'i's volcanoes. These high value woods can serve as the basis for a woodworking industry that can provide good paying, high skill jobs indefinitely if sustained yield forestry is practiced. A further benefit is habitat restoration to aid the plight of the many Hawaiian plants and animals on the endangered species list.

photo by D. Reed

Mauna Kea from Hilo Bay, island of Hawai'i

Another new agricultural venture in Hawai'i is the growing of timber bamboo. This giant grass exceeds six inches in diameter when mature and has a strength to weight ratio that far surpasses steel. It will become a source of low cost housing material when treatment facilities are completed in the Puna district of the island of Hawai'i.

The twenty world-class observatories near the 13,796 foot summit of Mauna Kea are creating both economic and academic resources for the island of Hawai'i. The dry, clear air at this summit creates viewing opportunities so outstanding that astronomers must schedule viewing times years in advance.

The intangible qualities of Hawai'i that keep it a magnet for tourists and residents alike must be examined and protected if the economy of the islands is to continue in a sustainable fashion. What value do you put on a tropical sunset over a grove of coconut palms? What is the value of a swim in crystal clear waters? The natural beauty of the islands, along with its rich cultural heritage are recognized by many as the factors that give Hawai'i its unique appeal. How many tourists and resorts can the islands support without destroying these characteristics?

Carved images at Pu'uhonua o Hōnaunau
National Historical Park, Kona, Hawai'i

At the heart of these questions lies another question. Is Hawai'i truly developing an independent, self-sustaining economy or is it controlled by outside investors who have merely replaced the planters as the movers and shakers of Hawai'i? While there are no simplistic answers to these worthy questions, there are some rays of hope. For example, there is a tax on all real estate sales in Hawai'i in which the seller is not a resident of Hawai'i. While not eliminating land speculation, this law encourages ownership by residents. And measures are being taken to increase native Hawaiian land ownership, as will be examined in more detail in the next chapter. Immersion programs in the Hawaiian language have been established in many schools to encourage the growth of traditional Hawaiian culture.

It is not the purview of historians to predict the future. An examination of the Hawaiian sovereignty movement will be next. This growing movement will undoubtedly have a profound effect on the shape of Hawai'i in the new millennium.

Chapter 12
Sovereignty

Along with the influx of tourists came the deluge of new residents. Inevitably demand for land to house the increasing population would lead to the displacement of even more Hawaiians. On Oʻahu a group called Kōkua Kalama was formed in the early 1970's to protest yet another eviction resulting from burgeoning development. The group sparked a rise in activism that has continued to grow since that time. A group with an apt acronym A.L.O.H.A. - Aboriginal Lands of Hawaiian Ancestry - was formed in 1972, with the goal of protesting the overthrow of the monarchy nearly a century earlier.

Hawaiian pride was further strengthened when the Polynesian Voyaging Society launched the Hōkūleʻa in 1975. This re-creation of a traditional Polynesian double hulled voyaging canoe sailed to Tahiti in 1976 using only ancient wayfaring techniques. Additional double hulled canoes have been built in the ensuing years that have traveled throughout the Polynesian triangle and as far as Japan.

Kahoʻolawe, a small island off the coast of Maui, had been used as a bombing range by the U.S. Navy since World War II. In 1976 the Protect Kahoʻolawe Ohana was formed to stop the bombing and to protect the natural and cultural resources of the island. The group filed a successful suit in federal court and began an occupation movement to apply pressure on the federal government. Live fire training was finally ended for good by President George H. W. Bush in 1990. Jurisdiction of the island was transferred to the State of Hawaiʻi in 1994.

The Hawaiian language was in jeopardy of ceasing to exist as an active language by the 1970's. Back in 1896 the use of the Hawaiian language as a medium of instruction was outlawed. This law was not repealed until 1986. ʻAha Pūnana Leo, became an active participant in the restoration of the language when they established a Hawaiian language pre-school system in 1984, inspired by the Maori language movement in New Zealand. This effort to strengthen and perpetuate the language has resulted in a proliferation of well attended Hawaiian immersion schools. Bolstered by strong support within the University of Hawai'i system there is a rapidly growing number of fluent Hawaiian speakers today. A PhD program in Hawaiian language is now offered at the University of Hawai'i at Hilo.

An unforeseen offshoot of the boom in tourism was an increasing value placed upon Hawaiian art, dance, and music, that are viewed as exotic by visitors. The ensuing Hawaiian renaissance did not stop at mere reenactments to create photo opportunities for tourists. Authentic Hawaiian culture was now suddenly in high demand. Getting in touch with their roots is a pursuit shared by many native Hawaiians. It should not be surprising that one of the results of this revival is a renewed demand for increased autonomy.

One of the models that native Hawaiians examined in pressing their claims was the Alaska Native Claims Settlement Act created in 1970. This act had been drafted in the new state to deal with the rights of native Alaskans and resulted in large cash, as well as land settlements to the original inhabitants. It is ironic that the much earlier Hawaiian Homelands Act of 1920 had served as a model for the Alaskans during their deliberations.

The Hawaiian Homelands were established with 188,000 acres to create opportunities for homesteading by Native Hawaiians. Unfortunately much of the acreage that was put into the program was too arid for agriculture. Many of the best acres were leased out rather than made available for homesteads. By 1992 only 40,000 of the acres were being utilized for their original purpose. At that time there was still a waiting list of almost 25,000 Hawaiians seeking land. In order for much of the land to be usable, major expenditures needed to be made for reliable water supplies and utilities.

The Office of Hawaiian Affairs was created in 1978 by an amendment to the state constitution. Its purpose was to hold title to the land given to the state from the federal government at statehood. At annexation, in 1898, the United States had taken possession of the former crown and government lands of the monarchy. This land was established as a trust for native Hawaiians. In the midst of growing internal pressure a commission was created in 1983 by the federal government to study the issue of reparations to native Hawaiians. The commission examined little evidence beyond blatantly pro-American accounts of early Hawai'i history, and ruled against reparations. This announcement was greeted by a storm of indignation from a broad spectrum of Hawai'i citizens including the then powerful Senator Dan Inouye.

Incidents with homeless Hawaiians who moved into tent cities on beaches throughout the islands grabbed a great deal of media attention during the early 1990's. Rents were skyrocketing at this time and people were being evicted in large numbers. These individuals, who were referred to as the "beach people," brought the issue of the plight of native Hawaiians to the attention of all in a manner that could not be ignored.

As sovereignty groups with various agendas proliferated, a Constitutional Convention for a Hawaiian Nation was called in 1987. Representatives from all of the islands came together and drafted a constitution. They also elected Mililani Trask to the position of president of Ka Lāhui Hawai'i, The Hawaiian Nation.

In 1993, as the 100th anniversary of the overthrow of the monarchy approached, many groups thought that the time was right for a major push for sovereignty. The federal government gave these groups a great deal of ammunition with the passage of Public Law 103-150. This law, which President Clinton signed in November of 1993, was a formal apology to native Hawaiians from the government of the United States for the overthrow of the monarchy 100 years earlier. The law had extensive quotes from the report of President Cleveland to Congress, included in an earlier chapter of this book.

With all of these demands for change, the previously mentioned Office of Hawaiian Affairs has joined the battle to empower the native people of Hawai'i. However, since OHA is funded by the state legislature and is in fact an agency of the

Senator Daniel Kahikina Akaka

81

state of Hawai'i it is viewed by some of the sovereignty activists as having an inherent conflict of interest with efforts to free Hawaiians from state and federal control. OHA's problems were further magnified by a ruling by the Supreme Court of the United States in February, 2000. Harold "Freddy" Rice, a haole rancher whose family has resided in Hawaii since the 1830's, sued the state claiming that OHA elections allowing only native Hawaiians to vote were in violation of the 15th Amendment of the U.S. Constitution which prohibits discrimination in voting based on race. This court ruling in favor of Rice has raised a number of questions that are yet to be resolved. The Governor of Hawai'i declared that all registered voters are eligible to vote for members of the OHA Board as of the November 2000 elections. Non-native Hawaiians are also being allowed to run for seats on the OHA Board. The entire base of programs that are designed to provide support for native Hawaiians is now being called into question.

These fears were realized when a lawsuit was filed in September of 2000 in Federal Court on Oahu. This suit filed on behalf of a non-Hawaiian claims the entire Office of Hawaiian Affairs is unconstitutional because it discriminates against non-Hawaiians. This suit, handled by the same attorney who represented Rice in the case cited earlier, was unsuccessful.

A bill, supported by the Clinton Administration, was introduced into the United States Senate by Hawai'i Senator Daniel Akaka in the Summer of 2000. This bill titled "The Native Hawaiian Recognition Bill" creates a process within the framework of federal law for the Native Hawaiian community to organize a governing body for self determination and self-governance. The government to government relationship with the United States created by this bill would be similar to the relationship that exists with Native American tribes. The bill is intentionally vague to allow Native Hawaiians to create and elect their own governing body. Once this governing body is in place the U. S. Government can then transfer land, resources and assets dedicated to Native Hawaiians under existing law to the Native Hawaiian Governing Body. This would basically create a new system in which OHA would no longer be needed. With the retirement of Senator Akaka in January of 2013 the passage of this legislation will fall to the remaining members of the Hawaiian delegation in Washington D.C. In an effort to speed along this process of self governance the new Democratic governor, Neil Abercrombie, signed the Native Hawaiian Recognition Bill into law in 2011. This Law created the Native Hawaiian Roll Call Commission. The function of this commission will be to generate a roll of qualified and interested Native Hawaiians who will help to determine the course that the indigenous people of Hawaii can take to determine their own destiny.

The Hawaiian Sovereignty Advisory Commission, an offshoot of the OHA, called for a vote in 1996 to determine if delegates should be elected to a convention to plan the course of sovereignty. Ka Lahui called for a boycott of the election as it was controlled by the state of Hawai'i. Of the over 75,000 ballots mailed out to native Hawaiians throughout the world only 30,000 were returned. Of those who voted, 75% voted to create the convention. The commission has now disbanded and the state says that it will not pay for further elections or a convention. A non-profit group called Hā Hawai'i was formed to raise the estimated $8 million needed for elections and a convention. In an election staged by Hā Hawai'i on January 17, 1999 to choose delegates to a sovereignty convention less than 9% of Hawaiians who were eligible to vote cast a ballot. Many Hawaiian sovereignty activists boycotted the election. They stated that the whole process was still too closely tied to the state. Hā Hawai'i attributed the poor turnout to a lack of education of the Hawaiian people which led to confusion about the issues involved in the election. They have requested $ 1.9 million from the state Office of Hawaiian Affairs to finance the convention and public relations needed to get the word out to the Hawaiian people. It is their feeling that once the convention gets underway it will arouse the interest of all Hawaiians and people will begin to become more involved in the whole process. The Office of Hawaiian Affairs has countered that the low voter turnout is evidence that a convention is premature at this time.

A very different election is being called for by the sovereignty group called Kanoa, to elect the rightful government of Hawai'i. They feel that the "Bayonet Constitution" that was forced upon King Kalākaua in 1887 is the rightful constitution of the Islands since the government of the United States has already admitted the 1893 revolution was not lawful in Public Law 103-150 which passed in 1993. The group is calling for the election of 24 members to the House of Nobles, and the election of a king or queen to head the government. Their plan would allow non-native Hawaiians to vote in the election as long as they pledge their allegiance to this "lawful government" of Hawai'i.

Hawaiian Sovereignty March in Honolulu

One of the major points of disagreement between the various groups working for Hawaiian sovereignty is the form that sovereignty should take if it is in fact enacted. There are three forms that could be taken and an infinite number of variables that could be implemented within any one of the three.

The first form would be modeled on the system most common in tribes of Native Americans. Sovereignty is limited to specific areas with the federal government maintaining ultimate control. Almost all of these treaties were established over 100 years ago. With the present legal resources available to them native Hawaiians could undoubtedly draft an agreement that would be more favorable to their interests than the treaties drafted during the 1800's and earlier by native tribes in the continental U.S.

The second option is quite a bit more complicated. Under this form native Hawaiians would be granted autonomous units within the state of Hawai'i. These units would be self governing including the right of taxation. This would provide the revenue source to establish successful communities without the need for government handouts and the strings which typically accompany them. Present lands controlled by OHA would be the obvious starting point to decide where these units might be located. The island of Kaho'olawe would be another source of land for Hawaiian occupation, once all of the unexploded ordnance is removed from this former Naval bombing range. How these units would interact with the state and federal government would require detailed negotiations. Ka Lahui has estimated that between Hawaiian Homelands and Crown Lands, that were taken by the Republic of Hawai'i and acquired by the U.S. at annexation, almost one and three-quarter million acres should be available.

The third, and most intimidating option for non-natives, is complete independence from the United States. While some dismiss this option as unattainable, it would not necessarily be as catastrophic a change as one might imagine. The U.S. Navy could still lease Pearl Harbor as they did in the time before territorial status. The tourist infrastructure would not be dismantled as the new government would recognize this major source of income. In the age of expanding democracy it is unlikely that the islands would return to a traditional monarchy. Issues such as who would be eligible for citizenship would warrant careful examination. There is no reason to assume that total independence would result in the creation of a system that would be unpalatable to all non-native Hawaiians.

The process of attaining sovereignty is a slow one. All of the groups have made their proposals in intentionally vague terms so, regardless of which system is chosen, there will still be plenty of room for compromise. Whatever form sovereignty may finally take, there are still a multitude of decisions to be made. At some point these proposals will need to be examined by the federal and state governments, and all current residents of the islands, both non-native citizens and native Hawaiians. This will begin a process of negotiation that, hopefully, will not lead to violence against person or property. Good faith and patience are attributes that will be required of all for a satisfactory resolution to issues unresolved since 1893.

Chapter 13
Hawai'i Enters the 21st Century

The lengthy Democratic Party monopoly on power in Hawai'i was ended in 2002 with the election of Republican Linda Lingle as governor. It was widely perceived that the Democrats had been in power for such a long time that widespread corruption was inevitable, leading to an upset victory by the Republicans. Apparently the dissatisfaction was far from a sweeping movement, proven when voters again elected a Democratic majority to both houses of the state legislature as well as maintaining the all Democratic Hawai'i delgation to the United States Congress. This flirtation with a Republican governor was relatively short lived. In 2010 Democrat Neil Abercrombie was elected governor with almost 60% of the vote. In this election that swept the GOP to control of the U.S. House of Representatives the number of Republicans reached an all time low in the Hawai'i State Senate with only one Republican elected to this body of 25 members.

The 2012 elections in Hawai'i were closely watched as what looked to be a tight race for the Senate seat vacated by retiring Senator Daniel Akaka was developing. With the U.S. Senate up for grabs the Republican party poured a lot of money into the campaign of former Governor Linda Lingle against her Democratic opponent Mazie Hirono. On election day however voters elected Hirono by a 25% margin. Hirono became the first female Senator from Hawai'i and the nation's first Asian-American woman Senator. She served six years in the U.S. House of Representatives and as Lieutenant Governor of Hawai'i from 1994-2002. With the governer's appointment to fill the Senate seat of the late Daniel Inouye, Lieutenant Governor Brian Schatz became the senior member of the Hawai'i delegation. In the race for the U.S. House of Representatives seat vacated by Hirono, Tulsi Gabbard, the Democratic candidate, easily won the election. Gabbard is the first American Samoan, the first Hindu, and one of the first female veterans in Congress. She joined Representative Colleen Hanabusa, thus

Hawai'i retained its solid four person Democratic delegation in the U.S. Congress.

A new focus of attention was placed on Hawai'i with the election of Barack Obama to the presidency of the United States of America in November of 2008. Obama received 76% of the vote in his birth state, by far his largest margin of victory. In the hotly contested 2012 presidential election President Obama again easily carried Hawai'i. Barack Hussein Obama was born in Honolulu in 1961. His parents were students at the University of Hawai'i. His mother came from Kansas and his father was from a rural region of Kenya. His parents were divorced when he was three years old and he moved to Indonesia with his mother and stepfather at the age of six. He returned to Hawai'i in 1971 with his mother and younger sister, Maya.

REUTERS/Larry Downing

President Obama giving the Punahou School Band the "shaka sign" during the 2009 Inaugural Parade.

While his mother and sister would leave Honolulu in 1977, Barack remained in the care of his grandparents until his completion of high school. Attending the prestigious Punahou School from grades 5 through 12, the multicultural world of Hawai'i undoubtedly helped to shape Barack's world view. One of only three black students, he graduated with honors in 1979. He remained very close to his grandparents and returned frequently for visits. Despite his grandmother's death just a few days before he was elected president, Obama retains strong roots in the state and returns every Christmas for an extended visit with relatives and friends from his youth.

The waves of change that have swept over the world from collapsing financial markets to fears of global warming have been felt in Hawai'i as well as the rest of the country. As you are by now aware the islands are unique in many ways and these new problems can truly be viewed as opportunities for the state of Hawai'i.

As tourism declines in the wake of rising fuel prices and a reduction in disposable income, the state is being forced to diversify its economy into new areas. Though painful choices must be made at present, this increased diversity can only help to provide us with a more sound and balanced economic base in future years. Let us explore some of the rapidly evolving issues in our state.

It is interesting to note that one of the main items on President Obama's agenda is energy independence and Hawai'i is taking the lead in pursuing alternative energy sources. At present Hawai'i is the state most dependent on petroleum in the United States with over 90% of our energy needs being met by oil. This is due largely to the fact that we have no locally produced sources of natural gas or coal. A positive statistic shows that, as of 2009, Hawai'i leads the U.S. in alternative energy with 7% of our energy coming from alternative sources. While this is a small percentage, the U.S. average is only 2% from non fossil fuel sources. The state has recently contracted with the federal department of energy to provide 40% of our energy from renewable sources by 2030. The state's Department of Business, Economic Development and Tourism has set an even more ambitious goal of 70% renewable use by 2030. The major sources of renewable energy in the state are geothermal, hydroelectric, wind, and solar, all of which the state has in abundance. There is even a suggested plan to cool downtown Honolulu high-rise buildings by recirculating cold ocean water through the buildings which would make electric air conditioning unneeded. As few of these buildings are more than a mile from the coast this seems like a feasible plan. This is just one example of using new local methods to reduce our energy dependence.

Another source of alternative energy that has been gaining momentum in Hawai'i is biodiesel. Biodiesel can be produced in one of two ways. The first is by recycling cooking oil from deep fryers in restaurants. A small Maui company started creating this type of biodiesel and then rented a fleet of VW bugs powered by the fuel years ago. Their efforts have expanded dramatically in recent years. Biodiesel can also be produced by growing crops high in oil such as oil palms. A new company is starting construction of a production facility on Maui that could produce 40 million gallons of biodiesel yearly with 120 million gallons possible at full build out. This biodiesel is already contracted to be sold to Maui Electric for electricity production. As supplies become available the facility will use 100% locally produced vegetable matter for their production. The long growing season in Hawai'i makes biofuels even more attractive. At full production this biodiesel could meet all of Maui's current power needs.

Hawai'i is taking the lead in the development of electric cars to wean the state further from petroleum. The legislature recently passed a law requiring all large parking facilities to have spaces allotted for recharging electric cars. Unfortunately the utilization of electric cars in the islands has been slowed considerably by the fact that major auto manufacturers have introduced and marketed electric car models mainly in the large markets on the East and West coasts.

The other side of energy issues is the reduction of greenhouse gases. As an island state there is a growing awareness of the potential impacts of global warming and rising sea levels. Hawai'i was the second state after California to pass a bill mandating a reduction in the production of greenhouse gases in 2007. This was followed up in 2009 with the creation of a Global Warming Task Force to begin long term planning for the steps that need to be taken to minimize the impacts of global climate change.

If Hawai'i sounds like a very "green" state this should not come as a surprise. With its strong dependance on tourism as the driving force of the economy, and the fact that tourism in Hawai'i is driven by its image of clean air, clean water and scenic natural beauty, it only makes sense that a pristine environment is a marketable asset. There is a recognition in many members of the business community that sound environmental policy creates jobs rather than eliminating them. Environmental protections play right into present concerns with sustainability in the islands.

Every state in the nation is talking about sustainability these days, but nowhere is it more important than in Hawai'i. As an island state located over 2,000 miles from the mainland special issues arise here. With a limited land base and many resources in short supply Hawai'i is particularly vulnerable to disruptions in the global economy and is making efforts to be more self-sufficient. Even a short term disruption of maritime shipping caused by a labor dispute can have wide spread ramifications in the islands. When you consider the large ranches on the island of Hawai'i and the groves of fruit trees and truck gardens on all of the islands it seems like we are growing plenty of food. It is surprising, therefore, that we grow only around 15% of the food that is consumed in the state. With a year round growing season and plenty of agricultural land left fallow by the collapse of the sugar and pineapple industries there is certainly a great deal of potential. The rapid increase in fuel prices has also raised the cost of shipping food to the islands, another reason for increased local production. "Buy local" is a slogan that we are hearing frequently and the abundance of well attended farmers' markets leads one to believe that change is coming.

Increased self-sufficiency will require major changes in land allocation to food production and increased marketing of locally grown food. With its many diverse ecosystems it is possible to grow cool weather crops such as apples and broccoli as well as the traditional tropical foodstuffs. As in all aspects of production, the economy of scale comes into play. It is obviously cheaper to import many foods from agribusiness producers than to grow them in Hawai'i. Even in the area of fruit production less than one-third of the fruit consumed in the islands is grown here. For a while young cattle from ranches in the islands were shipped to Canada to be fattened up in industrial feedlots and then the processed beef was shipped back to Hawai'i. Increased fuel prices have played a role in, at least temporarily, ending this triangle game. Until the full cost of food production including fuel cost, greenhouse gas creation, and food supply vulnerability are taken into account it is a hard sell to push increased agriculture. Recent increases in unemployment have created a large number of willing workers. This labor force could be employed in a redefined agricultural system with increased emphasis on local food production and less focus on export crops such as macadamia nuts and coffee. There is some opposition to the growing of biofuels, mentioned earlier, by individuals who are convinced that it is more important to use the land for growing food crops. Many of the issues raised in sustainability debates are far from simple, as there are multiple uses for all of our natural resources.

In trying to get a handle on the whole issue of sustainability the state commissioned a task force to come up with a plan to make Hawai'i more self sufficient in coming years. An elaborate document was drafted after over a year of town hall meetings and legislative hearings. The Hawai'i 2050 Sustainability Plan is almost 100 pages long, and examines many aspects of life in the state over the next 40 years. Not surprisingly, the plan calls for an increase in the production of locally grown foods, more use of renewable energy systems, and increased emphasis on high tech industries with yet another call to update our school system to provide the needed skilled labor.

High tech has real potential here in Hawai'i. We have never been able to compete in the manufacturing industries for several reasons. There is a shortage of traditional raw materials for production, such as iron ore or coal; the cost of shipping raw materials to Hawai'i would be too great; and the cost of shipping out manufactured goods to other markets would be far too costly. High tech industries do not have any of these constraints. Both the raw material (knowledge) and the finished products, be they software, architectural plans, or artistic creations, can be shipped in or out via the internet. The Islands' location in the middle of the Pacific Ocean is a real plus when face to face meetings are required between North American and Asian investors and developers.

An excellent example of how high tech can work in Hawai'i are the observatories located on top of Mauna Kea mentioned earlier in this book. The data generated by these observatories is analyzed by astronomers in all of the developed nations of the world. A new telescope proposed for the summit is The Thirty Meter Telescope, called the TMT. This will be by far the

Artist's Conception of The Thirty Meter Telescope on Mauna Kea
Courtesy of TMT Observatory Corporation. Image by Todd Mason

largest telescope in the world. Cal Tech is taking the lead in the proposal but universities and investors from Asia, the United States, and Europe are involved. There have been on-going disputes with some native Hawaiians and environmentalists over the management of the summit of what is a sacred mountain to Hawaiians. A comprehensive management plan has been developed to address these concerns.

Though every state in the nation is seeking high tech companies, Hawai'i seems to be making real progress. In 2004 Hawai'i was rated 39th in terms of tech sector growth. By 2008 we had moved up to 28th. For a small state this is very impressive. When you consider the quality of life benefits of island living our competitive advantage is increased considerably.

One of the first aspects of high tech to be felt in Hawai'i was the number of highly trained individuals who have relocated to Hawai'i while continuing to work for mainland firms by telecommuting, in this case on the internet. In my small neighborhood on the rural Puna coast on the island of Hawai'i there are individuals who do graphic design for a company in Vancouver, British Columbia, architectural work for California firms, consulting to the film industry, and of course the ubiquitous day traders who telecommute to Wall Street. These individuals are all contributing to Hawai'i's economy in ways that would be hard to imagine only 10 years ago.

Another bright spot for the future of Hawai'i is the large number of baby boomers who are choosing to retire in Hawai'i. For the most part these individuals are well educated and relatively affluent. The state has seen this wave coming and pensions are now free from state income taxes in Hawai'i. Many of these individuals are still relatively young and have a lot to contribute to the state through volunteer activities and service. Somebased their decision to relocate at least partially on the high value that they place on the cultural aspects that make these islands unique. It would not surprise me if they become some of the most ardent supporters of Hawaiian immersion programs that keep the culture vibrant and alive.

Recently efforts are being made to customize tourist experiences to meet the specialized needs of many travelers. The state bureaucracy has begun to realize that you can only go so far in marketing palm trees, beautiful beaches, and tropical sunsets. This old style industrial tourism is yielding to more independent travelers with special goals. One of these niche markets is wellness tourism. With the relative aging of the populations in most developed nations this is a market that is bound to grow over the years. With Hawai'i's large population of individuals of Asian ancestry there has always been increased demand for alternative modalities such as acupuncture and herbal medicine. Add to this the abundance of opportunities for massage, reiki, and cranial sacral therapies to name just a few. There is rapidly growing production of organic foods and range-fed meat products. Resorts are beginning to spring up that combine healthy local foods, alternative health specialists, and a relaxed pace of life, creating a truly restorative experience for guests - a major change from vacation styles that require you to rest up after you return home. On the other end of the vacation spectrum are high energy ecotourism adventures. These vacations can include hiking, kayaking, mountain biking, challenge courses, zip lines, and other high adrenaline activities. The underlying Hawaiian culture gives added appeal to a variety of specialty tourism.

As Hawai'i passes 50 years of statehood there are many rays of hope for the future potential of the 50th state. The diversity of Hawai'i stemming from its multitude of cultures, skills, natural ecosystems, and opportunities can only aid the options for meeting the ever changing possibilities of the 21st century. In the words of Mark Twain, the promise of the new millennium can be realized in "the loveliest fleet of islands that lies anchored in any ocean."

For further reading . . .

Beckwith, Martha. *Hawaiian Mythology*. Honolulu: University of Hawai'i Press, 1970.

Cordy, Ross. *Exalted Sits the Chief, The Ancient History of Hawai'i Island*. Honolulu: Mutual Publishing, 2000.

Daws, Gavan. *Honolulu, The First Century, The Story of the Town to 1876*. Honolulu: Mutual Publishing, LLC, 2006.

Daws, Gavan. *Land and Power in Hawaii*. Honolulu: University of Hawai'i Press, 1985.

Daws, Gavin. *Shoal of Time: A History of the Hawaiian Islands*. Honolulu: University of Hawai'i Press, 1974.

Fornander, Abraham. *Ancient History of the Hawaiian People*. Honolulu: Mutual Publishing, 1996

Handy, E.S. Craighill and Pukui, Mary Kawena. *The Polynesian Family System in Ka'ū, Hawai'i*. Honolulu: Mutual Publishing, 1998.

Howes, Craig and Osorio, Jon. *The Value of Hawai'i*. Honolulu: University of Hawai'i Press, 2010

Kamakau, Samuel M. *Ka Po'e Kahiko, The People of Old*. Honolulu: Bishop Museum Press, 1964

Kamakau, Samuel M. *Na Hana a ka Po'e Kahiko, The Works of the People of Old*. Honolulu: Bishop Museum Press, 1976

Kamakau, Samuel M. *Ruling Chiefs of Hawaii*. Honolulu: Kamehameha Schools Press, 1992

Kame'eleihiwa, Lilikala. *Native Land and Foreign Desires*. Honolulu: Bishop Museum Press, 1992.

Kane, Herb Kawainui. *Ancient Hawai'i*. Kawainui Press, 1997.

King, Samuel P. and Roth, Randall W. *Broken Trust: Greed, Mismanagement and Political Manipulation at America's Largest Charitable Trust*. Honolulu: University of Hawai'i Press, 2006.

Kirch, Patrick Vinton. *A Shark Going Inland is My Chief: The Island Civilization of Ancient Hawai'i*. University of California Press, 2012.

Kuykendall, Ralph S. *The Hawaiian Kingdom, Vol. 1, 2, 3.* , Honolulu: University of Hawai'i Press, 1938, 1965

Lili'uokalani, Queen. *Hawai'i's Story by Hawai'i's Queen*. Honolulu: Mutual Publishing, LLC, 1990.

Malo, David. *Hawaiian Antiquities, Mo'olelo Hawai'i*. Honolulu: Bishop Museum Press, 1951

Mitchell, Donald D.Kilolani. *Resource Units in Hawaiian Culture, Revised Edition*. Honolulu: Kamehameha Schools Press, 1992.

Silva, Noenoe K. *Aloha Betrayed, Native Hawaiian Resistance to American Colonialism*. Duke University Press, 2004.

Van Dyke, Jon M. *Who Owns the Crown Lands of Hawaii?* Honolulu: University of Hawai'i Press, 2008.

Glossary

ahi - yellow fin tuna
'āina - land
ahupua'a - system of land division that includes land from the coast to the mountains
akua - lesser gods
ali'i - royalty in the monarchy system
ali'i nui - high chief
aloha - greeting, love, sharing,
a'u - marlin, swordfish
'aumākua - ancestral spirits
grinds - food
hala - pandanus tree
hale - house or home
hānai - adopted
haole - foreigner, white person
hapa - one-half, person of mixed blood
Hawai'i ne'i - Hawaiian islands
heiau - ancient Hawaiian temple
hui - group, partnership, club
hula - dance, used in oral history
'ili - land section within ahupua'a
imu - underground oven
issei - first generation Japanese
kāhili - feathered staff of ali'i
kahuna - learned professional, priest
kama'āina - long time resident
kanaka - native born Hawaiian
Kanaloa - god of the sea, underworld
Kāne - chief god of Hawaiian religion
kane - man
kapu - taboo, forbidden, sacred
kapu moe - prostration taboo
keiki - child, children, young plant
koa - valuable hardwood tree, acacia
kōkua - help out, cooperation
kona - leeward coast
kōnane - game like checkers
Kūkailimoku - Hawaiian god of war

kuhina nui - prime minister
kuleana - family land holding
kūpuna - grandparents or elders
lānai - porch or deck
lei - flower garland
liliko'i - passion fruit
limu - seaweed, underwater plants
Lono - god of the makahiki, harvest
lū'au - large feast
luna - overseer, as on a plantation
mahalo - thanks, gratitude
maka'āinana - commoner
Makahiki - harvest festival
makai - toward the sea
malihini - newcomer
malo - loincloth worn by men
manō - shark
mauka - towards the mountains
mele - song, chant
Menehune - race of small people
nisei - second generation Japanese
'ohana - extended family
'ono - tasty, delicious
Pākē - Hawaiian for Chinese
pali - cliff
paniolo - cowboy
pau hana - finished with work
Pelehonuamea - deity of volcanoes
poi - food staple made from taro
pono - goodness, righteous
sansei - third generation Japanese
tapa - kapa, cloth made from paper mulberry bark
taro - kalo, crop grown for food
ti - kī, woody plant with many uses, leaves are used in cooking
tutu - grandparent
'ukulele - musical instrument with four strings. Lit. "leaping flea"
wahine - woman

Index

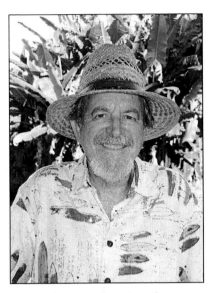

About the Author

Dr. Phil Barnes has been an educator for the past thirty years. During this period he has taught students from the intermediate grades through grad school. His background includes study in both biology and history. He received his bachelors degree from Purdue University, his masters from Indiana University, and two doctoral level degrees from the University of Miami. He is an active member of the Sierra Club and has served on the executive board of the local Moku Loa group for almost ten years. Hawaiian Historical Society, Hawaii Ecotourism Association and is listed in "Who's Who Among America's Teachers." Phil is a member of the Kamehameha Canoe Club and is enjoying the official state sport of outrigger canoe racing. He has taught Hawaiian Studies courses for over ten years. He and his wife, Diane, make their home in Kehena Beach on the Island of Hawai'i.

Books published by the PETROGLYPH PRESS